Wonders of
VENICE

The story of a unique city
in a brand new illustrated guide

Venice and the Islands of **Burano, Murano, Torcello**
and the **Lido**

The **Venetian cuisine** - The **carnival** masks
FREE: an enchanting journey through the canals
to discover and remember Venice

LOZZI EDITORI

SUMMARY

INTRODUCTION...5

HISTORY OF VENICE..8

THE GRAND CANAL 13

SAN MARCO 45

SAN POLO 85

SANTA CROCE 105

CANNAREGIO...111

DORSODURO AND GIUDECCA 121

CASTELLO 135

ISLANDS (Murano, Burano, Torcello, Lido) 147

SAILING ALONG THE GRAND CANAL...........159

THE MASK OF THE VENICE CARNIVAL 181

VENETIAN CUISINE.......................................189

Lozzi Editori s.r.l.
Via Aurelia 424
00165 Roma
Tel. 0039 06 88970491
e-mail: info@lozzieditori.com
website: www.lozzieditori.com

Texts by: Alessandra Rossi
Photographs: Archivio Arsenale Editore,
Mark Smith, (18, 22-23, 43, 64), Francesco Nannarelli (21, 103)
Translation: Sarah Jane Nodes

The publisher undertakes to carry out the necessary provisions for photos
of uncertain provenance

Graphic design and page layout: Arsenale Editore
Printed in March 2012 by
Editoriale Bortolazzi Stei Srl, San Giovanni Lupatoto (VR)

wonders of
VENICE

Venice is, first and foremost, the most beautiful city in the world. A unique city, a finely carved jewel, emerging as if by magic from the water and remaining suspended between sky and land to recount an ancient history of splendour and power, but also a lively and joyous present. Venice: the city of the doges, with its canals and its gondolas; the city of Vivaldi, of Marco Polo and of Giacomo Casanova; a continuous source of marvels and contradictions, where every corner, every perspective is full of emotion and poetry and where no one can remain unmoved. You wander through Venice soaking in this atmosphere, adapting to its pace, slowed down by its urban conformation. You might suddenly come across St. Mark's basilica, built to house the body of the city's patron, the very symbol of the power of the Most Serene Republic, or the magnificent Palazzo Ducale, home to the doges, or maybe the Rialto Bridge, the Punta della Dogana, the church of San Giorgio and the church of the Salute and in all the magnificent palaces lining the Grand Canal. After all these sights you just have to let this timeless atmosphere envelop you, to discover what Camillo Boito described as "a garland of fragrant flowers.... a necklace of precious stones... a fairy, who attracts and enchants you".

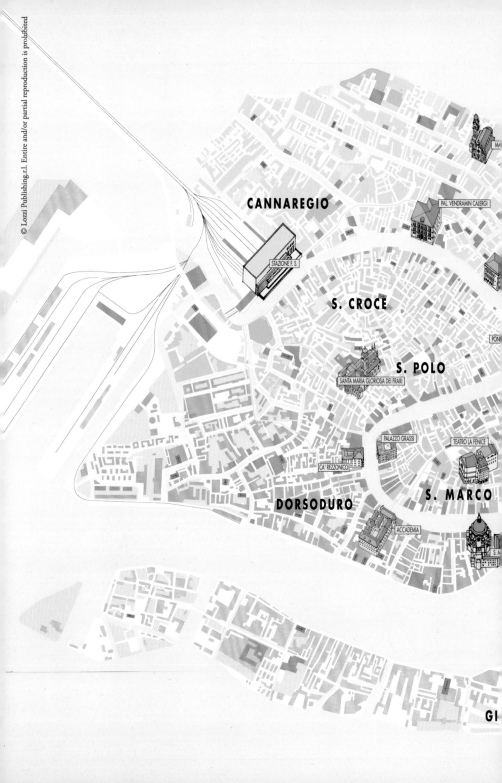

CANNAREGIO

STAZIONE F. S.

S. CROCE

PAL. VENDRAMIN CALERGI

S. POLO

SANTA MARIA GLORIOSA DEI FRARI

PON

PALAZZO GRASSI

TEATRO LA FENICE

CA' REZZONICO

DORSODURO

S. MARCO

ACCADEMIA

GI

CITY MAP

ISOLA DI
SAN MICHELE

SS. GIOVANNI E PAOLO

MIRACOLI

PONTE DEI SOSPIRI **CASTELLO**

ISOLA DI
SAN GIORGIO
MAGGIORE

SANT'ELENA

THE FIRST SETTLEMENTS

Venice has an official birthday. It is 25 March 421, the feast of the Annunciation, when, according to tradition, the population fleeing from the barbarian invasions established the first settlement on the islands of the lagoon and founded the church of San Giacometto on the Riva Alta (Rialto). At that time "Venice" was just an unhealthy swamp, whose few inhabitants eked a living by fishing and salt production. It was only in the 5th century that the people of the hinterland, threatened by the barbarians, and in particular the Huns (452) and the Longobards (568), came down to the lagoon, leaving the undefended countryside behind (such as Altinum and Concordia Sagittaria). It was from this time that the term Venetia, once referred to all of Veneto, came to indicate the area of the lagoons still in Byzantine hands. The Byzantines realized its strategic importance and in 697 built the Duchy of Venice, subject to Constantinople and, in particular, to the Exarchate of Ravenna, with its capital first at Heracliana, then Metamauco and, after 821, in the more secure Rialto.

❶ *Prospect of Venice, Castello del Buonconsiglio, Trento.*
❷ *Imaginary reconstruction of Venice, Biblioteca Marciana.*
❸ *Imaginary view of St Mark's Basin in a miniature from the Marco Polo codex, Oxford Bodleian Library (14th century).*

THE CITY TAKES SHAPE

It was in the 13th century that some sixty parishes started to join forces. Each parish corresponded to an island where, besides a church and some houses and palaces, there was a market, a small port and fields for animals and growing crops. The islands were linked by ferries or by footbridges. Each island was an autonomous unit, but they constituted a single territory under a government which had already started to claim its independence from Ravenna in the 9th century.

The city still maintained a special relationship with Byzantium and the Orient as a whole and this, together with its vicinity to the empire, made it one of the main trading ports between the West and East. A dynamic and enterprising merchant class soon developed which, over four centuries, transformed the city into a world-class power, capable of ruling the seas and dictating its rules to all Europe.

❹ *Francesco Bassano the younger, Alexander III Presenting the Sword to Doge Ziani, Doge's Palace, Sala del Maggior Consiglio.*
❺ *Gentile Bellini, Procession in Piazza San Marco, Gallerie dell'Accademia.*

THE MARITIME CITIES

Amalfi, Genoa, Pisa and Venice are the best-known Italian maritime republics, so called in the 19th century to define the powerful marine cities famous throughout the world since the year 1000.

The maritime cities' main characteristics were their political autonomy, their own money accepted throughout the Mediterranean basin and, above all, their participation in the Crusades with their own fleet. There were thus many Mediterranean marine cities (for example Ancona, Gaeta, Noli, Ragusa, Trani); but since World War II the definition has generally been restricted to the cities bearing the Italian navy flag in their coats-of-arms, and that is Amalfi, Genoa, Pisa and Venice.

THE SPLENDOUR OF THE MOST SERENE REPUBLIC

The fortune of Venice comes from its position, the rational exploitation of its natural resources, an efficient merchant fleet, the important concessions granted by Constantinople thanks to the protection of its ships in the Mediterranean, the participation in the Crusades and an extensive diplomatic network. These factors helped to establish an empire that, at the time of its greatest glory, extended from Bergamo in the north to the entire Dalmatian coast, right down to the Greek coast, including Corfu, part of the Peloponnese, Crete and Cyprus. In the 15th century, the territory of the Republic ran from the river Adda to Istria, and from part of the current province of Belluno to the lower Po Valley. A dominion in which Byzantine elements fitted harmoniously into a late Roman plan producing something truly unique and reaching the highest peaks in the history of humanity. In which the basilica of St. Mark, inspired by the church of the Twelve Apostles in Constantinople, was its most representative and majestic work.

❶ *Paris Bordon, The Presentation of the Ring to the Doge, Gallerie dell'Accademia.*
❷ *One of the lions in front of the Arsenal entrance.*
❸ *Canaletto, Piazza San Marco with the Basilica, Fogg Art Museum, Cambridge.*

THE DECLINE BEGINS

At the beginning of the 16th century Venice was one of the most important states in Europe, capable of withstanding the League of the Cambrai, risen under the papacy, the empire and France. Nonetheless the creation of the great European national states and the globalization of the maritime trade had considerably reduced Venice's power. The Republic was still continuing to exhibit its usual verve and ostentation right into in the 18th century but its decline was by now inevitable and evident. So, when on 12 May 1797 Napoleon entered the city with his army, not only did no one try to stop him but many believed that he was bringing new ideas of freedom and democracy. But the city only obtained the loss of its millenary independence and entered a difficult stage with the alternation of French and Austrian domination.

VENICE TODAY

Venice is today quite a small city with some 60,000 inhabitants, but stands in the centre of a much larger and more complex territory. It attracts hundreds of thousands of tourists all the year round, besides a sizable daily flow of commuters, students and workers.

The city has had to tackle many emergencies caused by its magnificent anomaly, starting with tidal levels and sinking, not to mention the dilapidated state of its residential buildings. In Venice a great many houses are empty or inhabited only for a few months a year, making it difficult to ensure efficient maintenance. The challenge Venice faces is that of continuing to be a living and lived in city full of bustling activities rather than a static museum-city sealed off from the world and history.

❷

❸

1 · The Grand Canal

THE GRAND CANAL

The Grand Canal has a unique significance. Whoever comes to Venice, whether to stay or just to visit, passes through it several times a day. Despite this, the continual passage of water buses, water taxis and gondolas does not manage to destroy Its enchantment. We will describe here some events that have made this waterway the symbol of Venice. Then on page 158 we propose an exceptional journey that will illustrate the facades lining the two sides of the Canal. It was along this waterway, dividing the city into two, that the first nucleus of Venice was born. The early wooden houses have given way to three thousand eight hundred metres of palaces, or better of *Ca'*. At the time of the Republic only the doge's residence could be called a palace, all the others were houses or *case*.

The "*fondaco*" houses were built for the foreign merchants and combined warehouse and residence; they were often flanked by defensive towers (*torreselle*), as in the **Fondaco of the Turks and the Fondaco of the Germans.** Byzantine influences instead created the Venetian-Byzantine style**,** characterized by its large loggias with round or elongated arches. Fine examples of this style are to be found in Ca' Farsetti, Ca' Loredan and Ca' Da Mosto.

The Dogana Da Mar was built in the 17th century as a customs house in a strategic position at the mouth of the Grand Canal. The building, by Benoni, has a triangular plan and is famous for its tower surmounted by a Golden Ball held by two Atlases. All this is topped by the statue called "Occasio" symbolizing fortune. In 2009, after a major restoration by Tadao Ando, the Dogana complex became an exhibition centre for François Pinault's modern art collection.

When the gothic appears in Venice, along the Grand Canal you start to see open marble fascias, often called *laces*, such as those decorating the Ca' d'Oro and Palazzo Bernardo.

Jacopo Sansovino was one of the major Renaissance architects working on the Grand Canal and the **Fabbriche Nuove in Rialto**, the **Ca' Granda** and **Palazzo Dolfin Manin** have facades with the typical horizontal layout and rounded arches. Instead, the Baroque is linked to the name of Baldassarre Longhena who designed, among others, the **Santa Maria della Salute church**, one of the main attractions of Canal Grande, **Ca' Pesaro and Ca' Rezzonico**. **San Simeon Piccolo and Palazzo Grassi** represent Venetian neo-classical architecture. The fall of the Republic in 1797 also had the effect of stopping the construction of housing on the Grand Canal, as symbolized by **San Marcuola** and **Palazzo Venier dei Leoni**, both unfinished. Italian Unification stimulated construction and new buildings such as the **Pescaria in Rialto** date back to this epoch, besides various restorations and reconversions.

THE HISTORICAL REGATTA

The Historical Regatta (*Regata Storica*), so called since 1889, dates back some six hundred years. It recalls the return to Venice in 1489 of Caterina Cornaro, a Venetian aristocrat who married James, King of Cyprus, and abdicated her throne in favour of the Republic. The arrival of the Queen of Cyprus is commemorated the first Sunday of September with a historical procession opening the traditional regatta: palaces, balconies and roof-terraces are hung with brocades, tapestries and damasks. Traditionally, some nobles threw terracotta balls (*balote*) from the bows of the parade galleys (b*issone*) to the more undisciplined boats to maintain order. Now the *bissone* are used only to open the historical procession. Dozens of typical 16th-century boats leave St. Mark's basin and throng the Grand Canal. They carry the doge, the *dogaressa*, Caterina Corner, nobles dressed in silk and brocade, ambassadors from the east and senators in a faithful reconstruction of the Serenissima Republic's glorious past. The actual regatta consists of various competitions in which the most popular is the **regata dei gondolini**. The race ends on the *machina*, a singular floating stand place in front of Ca' Foscari. Here the prizes in money and flags are handed out. The first to arrive is given a red flag, the second a white, the third a green and the fourth a blue flag. This latter used to be yellow and was decorated with a small pig, not known for its swiftness. The firework display at midnight on the Grand Canal provides a fitting end to the day.

GONDOLAS AND GONDOLIERS

Over the centuries becoming the symbol of the city, the origins of this very particular boat date back probably to 1100 (the first official document in which it is mentioned is a decree of doge *Vitale Falier* of 1094). 11 metres long and weighing some 600 kg, they can be easily handled by one person with one oar thanks to their manoeuvrability. The gondoliers who used to serve their master are now at the service of the tourists who can admire the beauty of the canals on a ride from the Ponte della Paglia. Often you find a *gansér* alongside the gondolas, someone who earns tips by pulling the boat to the edge and helping the passengers to get in and out.

Ca' Dario was commissioned by Giovanni Dario, a high-ranking Greek diplomat, at the end of the 15th century. It is famous not only for its fine Renaissance facade but also for the dramatic events in which many of its owners were involved since the 18th century.

Palazzo Falier Canossa with its two enclosed balconies, called liagò.
The dining room is lined with decorative mirrors.

Palazzo Grassi designed by Longhena on commission of the Grassi family, perhaps originating from Bologna. Since 2006 the palace has been owned by François Pinault who organizes art exhibitions here.

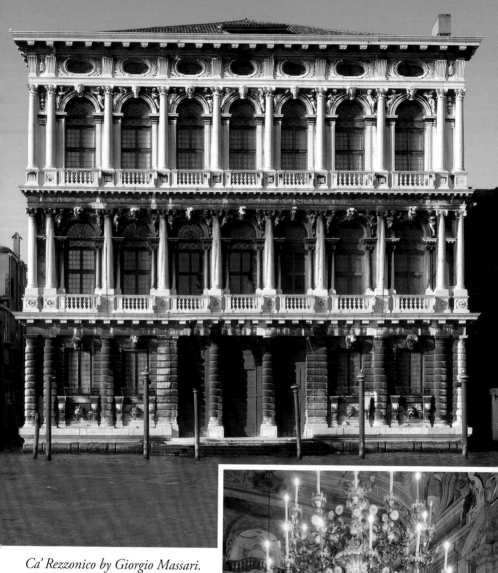

*Ca' Rezzonico by Giorgio Massari.
It houses the Venetian Museo
del Settecento with works by
Canaletto, Francesco Guardi,
Pietro Longhi, Tintoretto and
Tiepolo.*

Palazzo Morosini Sagredo. Inside, the 18th century grand staircase is by Tirali and is decorated with a fresco representing the Fall of the Giants by Pietro Longhi. The main reception room contains paintings by Andrea Urbani done in 1773.

Palazzo Corner della Regina. The name comes from Caterina Corner, heir to the crown of Cyprus. The gothic palace in which Caterina lived was demolished and a new one built in 1724.

SAN STAE

This medieval church dedicated to Saint Eustachius (San Stae in Venetian dialect), was reconstructed in 1678 by *Giovanni Grassi* who had it turned towards the Grand Canal. The facade has a single order with two lateral wings corresponding to the chapels inside. The entrance, framed by niches and bas reliefs, is topped by a tympanum full of complex statuary. The interior, with evident Palladian influences, is a wide rectangular nave with a barrel vault, three chapels on each side and a square presbytery reached by a few steps. This latter has fine examples of 18th-century paintings, with **St. James the Greater** by *Piazzetta*, the **Martyrdom of St. Bartholomew** by G*iambattista Tiepolo* and **Liberation of St. Peter by** *Sebastiano Ricci*.

CA' PESARO

The palace was constructed in the mid-17th century for the noble and wealthy Pesaro family. It was designed by the Venetian Baroque architect, *Baldassarre Longhena,* who is also responsible for the church of the Salute and Ca' Rezzonico. The facade on the Grand Canal is impressive and the vast entrance hall is equally magnificent. The palace is enriched with decorations and works by famous artists such as *Tiepolo, Carpaccio, Bellini, Giorgione, Titian and Tintoretto.* After the death of the last Pesaro in 1830, most of heritage was sold in auction in London. The palace then passed through various hands until it was acquired by the Duchess *Felicita Bevilacqua La Masa,* who gave it to the city to house Venice's **Museum of Modern Art**.

①

CA' D'ORO

Built between 1421 and 1443 for the rich Venetian merchant *Marino Contarini*, Ca' d'Oro (Golden House) is considered the finest example of *floral gothic* on the Grand Canal. Its name comes from the splendid gilt, red and ultramarine decorations which once adorned its facade.

❶ *View of the Grand Canal from Ca' d'Oro.*

❷ *The facade of Ca' d'Oro, magnificent example of floral gothic.*

❸ *The courtyard of Ca' d'Oro in Istrian stone with its historic well.*

②

③

The Fondaco dei Turchi was built in the early 13th century. The palace later became the property of the Serenissima and was often used to receive illustrious personages. It now contains the Museo di Storia Naturale.

Palazzo Belloni Battagia, with a facade designed by Baldassare Longhena.

SAN SIMEONE PICCOLO

The church, dedicated to the apostles Simon and Judas, was built between 1718 and 1738 by *Giovanni Scalfarotto* on the site of a 9th-century building. It is very visible thanks both to its high dome and its position in front of the railway station, on the other side of the Grand Canal. The circular design represents one of the first examples of Italian neoclassical architecture. Inside there is a fine **Last Supper** by *Tintoretto*.

Palazzo Loredan Vendramin Calergi, now housing the Venice Casino.

ACCADEMIA BRIDGE

From this bridge you have the best view of the Grand Canal: on one side San Marco and Santa Maria della Salute, on the other the various palaces overlooking the water, among which Palazzo Balbi stands out.

The bridge was initially built in iron in 1854 and designed by the engineer *Neville*; because of its dangerous condition it was demolished and replaced by a temporary wooden bridge in 1932, still in place today.

RIALTO BRIDGE

The oldest remains of the village of Rivoaltus established on the banks of the Rio Businiacus (the future Grand Canal), destined to become the first "district" of Venice, date back to the 9th century.

The overcrowding of the west bank pushed the population towards the sea, creating the area of San Marco and making it necessary to have a constant link between the two banks. The first rudimental crossing consisted of a pontoon bridge built in 1181. It was only in 1250 that a wooden bridge appeared with two inclined ramps meeting at a mobile central section that could be raised to allow the passage of tall ships. The first proposal for a stone bridge dates back to 1503, and architects such as *Jacopo Sansovino*, *Andrea Palladio* and *Vignola* provided designs for it in 1551 but it was not until 1591 that the present bridge by *Antonio da Ponte* was built. The structure, consisting of a single span 7.5 metres high and 28 metres across, is similar to the previous wooden one: inclined ramps lead up to a central portico with rows of shops on each side, with a central section framing the Grand Canal, pulsing heart and precious emblem of Venice.

SCALZI BRIDGE

An initial bridge was built in 1858 under the Hapsburg domination. It was an iron truss structure only four metres tall so that ships with masts could not pass underneath. The style was in strong contrast with the surrounding buildings. The deterioration of the iron forced the municipality to replace the metal bridge with a new one clad in Istrian stone with a single span, designed by *Eugenio Miozzi*. The work started on 4 May 1932 and the bridge was inaugurated just two years later, on 28 October 1934. It is set right in front of the railway station.

COSTITUZIONE BRIDGE

The Constitution Bridge, universally known by the name of its Spanish designer, *Calatrava*, was completed in 2008. It is a modern structure with a single span, supported by a central steel arch, painted red with glass parapets and pavement combined with traditional materials such as Istrian stone. The access steps are also in glass, which unfortunately means that the disabled and elderly have problems using the bridge. To overcome this a mobility lift system resembling cocoons holding two people has been designed. Another modern element is the underlit steps, although it was necessary to have additional spotlights in the access areas.

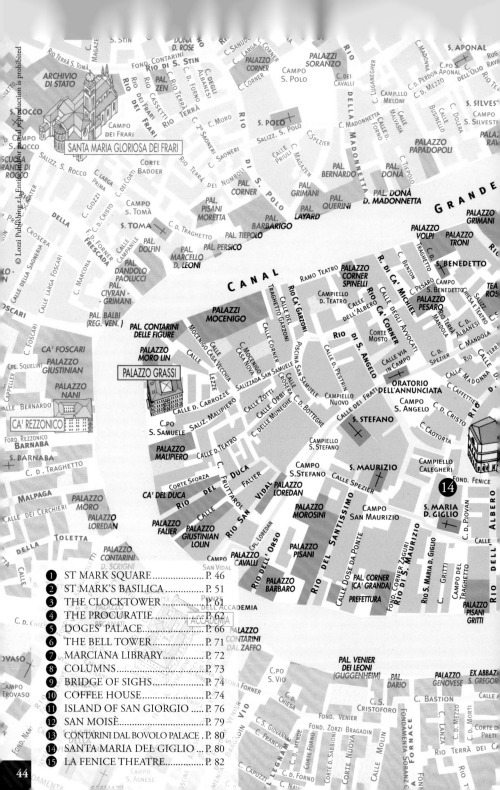

1. ST MARK SQUARE.................... P. 46
2. ST MARK'S BASILICA .... P. 51
3. THE CLOCKTOWER.................. P. 61
4. THE PROCURATIE .... P. 62
5. DOGES' PALACE..................... P. 66
6. THE BELL TOWER .... P. 71
7. MARCIANA LIBRARY............. P. 72
8. COLUMNS .... P. 73
9. BRIDGE OF SIGHS.................. P. 74
10. COFFEE HOUSE...................... P. 74
11. ISLAND OF SAN GIORGIO ..... P. 76
12. SAN MOISÈ .... P. 79
13. CONTARINI DAL BOVOLO PALACE . P. 80
14. SANTA MARIA DEL GIGLIO ... P. 80
15. LA FENICE THEATRE............... P. 82

PONTE DI RIALTO

CALLE D. MADONNA
CANA
DIECI SAVI
ERR
PONTE DI RIALTO
CALLE D. CINQUE
DOGANA DI TERRA
CALLE D. VIN
DELLO STORIONE DEL
Riva D. FERRO
SAN
BARTOLOMEO
CALLE
PALAZZO
MANIN
LARGA MAZZINI
PALAZZO
BEMBO
Rio DI
SCUOLA
S. TEODORO
S. SALVADOR
CALLE D. ACQUE
CALLE D. MEZZO
D. FERRO
CARBON
Calle Bembo
PALAZZO
DANDOLO
CALLE DEL TEATRO
CORTE
TEATRO
CALLE D. TEATRO
CALLE D. SCALE
S. SALVADOR
PISCINA S. ZULIAN
CALLE D. BALBI
S. ZULIAN
UNICIPIO
CARBON
SALIZZ.
S. LUCA
CAMPO
S. LUCA
CALLE D. MAGAZEN
CALLE D. MONTE DELLE BALLOTTE
SALVADOR
MERCERIA S. ZULIAN
S. ZULIAN
CAMPO
S. GUERRA
RIO
DI
S. ZULIAN
CALLE D. CASSELLARIA
PALAZZO
TASCA
PAPAFAVA
3
C. D. LOCANDE
SALIZZ.
S. PATERNIAN
FUSERI
GOLDONI
CALLE
CALLE D. GAMBARO
CALLE D. PIGNOLI
MERCERIA D. OROLOGIO
C. LARGA S. MARCO
PALAZZO
SORANZO
S. GIOVANNI
NOVO
L. CONTARINI
DEL BOVOLO
Rio
CALLE UNGHERIA
S. GALLO
RAMO S. GALLO
CALLE D. COLONNE
CALLE TERRÀ D. PRETI
CALLE FIUBERA
CALLE D. SPADARIA
PIZZETTA
DEI
LEONI
C. CANONICA
Ruga Giuffa
C. MALVASIA
Rio
FUSERI
FONDAM
S. GALLO
RAMO S. GALLO
S. GALLO
RIO D. PROCURATIE
3
MERC. D. PROCURATIE
2
S. MARCO
PONTE DEI SOSPIRI
C. D. BARCAROLI
C. VENIER
Calle Fuseri
CALLE DEI
P. D.
C. D. ZORZI
FONDAM. OREGOGIO
4
1
6
9
NTIN
Frezzaria
CALLE DEL CARRO
C. DEL SALVADEGO
5
PIAZZA
S. MARCO
PIAZZETTA
Marco
Piscina
S. Moisè
CALLE DEL BOGNOLO
C. VENEZIANA
BOCCA
DI PIAZZA
12
7
8
LARGA XXII Marzo S. Moisè
CORTE CONTARINA
SALIZZ. S. Moisè
C.PO
S. MOISÈ
PALAZZO
DUCALE
PONTE D.
PAGLIA
C. D.
CRISTO
BARCAROLI
Rio DEI
C. Barozzi
Calle del Ridotto
CALLE DEL CARRO
C. VALLARESSO
GIARDINI EX REALI
RIO DELLA ZECCA
MOLO
11
C. D. Barozzi
Calle 13 Martiri
Fondam. D. Farine
CAPITANERIA
DI PORTO
10
PALAZZO
TIEPOLO
PALAZZO
TREVES
DE' BONFILI

DOGANA
DI MARE

S. MARIA DELLA SALUTE

N 2
S. GIORGIO
C.ni
S. Giorgio
S. GIORGIO
MAGGIORE
FONDAZIONE
CINI
CAMPO
S. BARBARA
ISOLA DI
S. GIORGIO MAGGIORE
CANALE DELLA GRAZIA

1 • THE GRAND CANAL — P. 12

3 • SAN POLO — P. 84

4 • SANTA CROCE — P. 104

5 • CANNAREGIO — P. 110

6 • DORSODURO AND GIUDECCA — P. 120

7 • CASTELLO — P. 134

8 • ISLANDS — P. 146

ST MARK SQUARE

Symbol of the city and one of the most beautiful squares in the world, Piazza San Marco is the only real "square" in Venice since all the others are called "*campi*" (fields).

It has always been the political and religious centre of Venice. It has a trapezoidal shape and is framed by magnificent buildings such as St. Mark's Basilica, the Doges' Palace, the Clocktower, the Procuratie and the Campanile. The internationally famous annual Carnival also takes place here.

In the 11th century the square was about half its present size and ended in a small canal, beyond which stood the church of San Geminiano, now destroyed. The Piazzetta San Marco instead had a quay and the Doges' Palace was surrounded by water on four sides because a *rio* or stream separated it from the Basilica. During the following century the quay and *rio* were paved over with bricks laid in a herringbone pattern (the current pavement dates back to the first half of the 18th century). Piazza San Marco underwent a further restyling by *Jacopo Sansovino* in the 16th century.

ST MARK'S BASILICA

St Mark's Basilica has undergone numerous reconstructions over the centuries. In 832 a first basilica was built to house the remains of Mark the Evangelist from Alexandria. This first building was burnt down in 976 and then rebuilt in 978 by Doge *Pietro Orseolo I*. The current basilica dates back to a further reconstruction begun by *Domenico Contarini* in 1063, who copied the dimensions and plan of the previous building. The new consecration took place in 1094. Up to 1807, when it became the Cathedral of Venice, it was the Doges' Chapel where the major celebrations were held and the appointment of the doge consecrated.

The interior plan is based on a Greek cross, with the intersection and each arm emphasized by five large domes creating organic and dense spatial elements of columns and arches. It is a complex and multilayered structure, where Byzantine, Gothic and Romanesque influences make it difficult to trace the original layout (perhaps a basilica with a nave and two aisles). The splendid gold mosaic decoration inside the basilica was already in place at the end of the 12th century. By the first half of that century the narthex embracing the entire western arm had also been completed and the imposing facade could be created.

Above left: view of the five domes of St Mark's Basilica. The domes were made in perforated brick so the structure would be not be too heavy for land reclaimed from the lagoon.

Part of the loot sacked by the Venetians from Constantinople during the Fourth Crusade was a quadriga of four gilded bronze horses, placed in the centre of the facade (left). The horses have now been replaced by bronze replicas whereas the originals, restored in 1977, are kept in the Museo di San Marco.

Over the centuries the basilica was continually enriched with columns, friezes, marbles, sculptures and gold brought to Venice by merchants and crusaders. Particularly famous and precious was the loot sacked from Constantinople in the Fourth Crusade of 1204, now part of **St Mark's Treasure,** which also provided fabulous vestments, altar cloths and holy vessels. In the 13th century the original domes were covered with higher wooden, lead-covered domes and the precious mosaics were completed. However, it was only in the 15th century, with the decoration of the upper part of the facades that the current aspect of the basilica was achieved. The last interventions involved the **Baptistery** and **St Isidor of Chio's Chapel** (14th century), the **Sacristy** (15th century) and the **Zen Chapel** (16th century). The basilica was finally completed in 1617 when two altars were placed inside.

❶ *Detail of the facade with the portal and the quadriga.*
❷ *St Mark and the Lion above the central window.*
❸ *The lunette of the central portal of the Basilica with the Last Judgment.*
❹ *Two lunettes with episodes from the life of Christ: The Deposition from the Cross, Descent to the Underworld, Resurrection and Ascension.*

❶ The tetrarchs: 4 porphyry statues representing the Roman emperors of the East and West, sacked from Constantinople during the Fourth Crusade (1204).

❷ Detail of the back portal with dodecahedral in the pavement mosaic.

❸ and ❹ Details of the months of October and November in the bas-relief on the main portal.

❺ Pentecost dome inside the Basilica. At the top, in the middle of an aureole of concentric circles, the symbols of the throne, book and dove. Silver rays propagate light, communicating the Trinitarian life to the Twelve Apostles with tongues of fire above their heads

.

Page 56:

❶ Iconostasis separating the altar from the rest of the church; the sculptures depict the Madonna, St John and the Apostles flanked by a great gold and silver cross, a work by Jacopo di Marco Bennato.

❷ Ascension and Pentecost domes. In the first Christ, accompanied by the Madonna and the Apostles, sits on an arc of light illuminating the starry blue background.

❸ St Mark's crypt.

❹ The ciborium with the Golden Ball: this magnificent work in gold, silver and precious stones was made especially for the Basilica.

Page 58:

St Mark's Basilica with the piazza under water. In front of the Basilica the famous causeways for people to walk on.

①

②

③

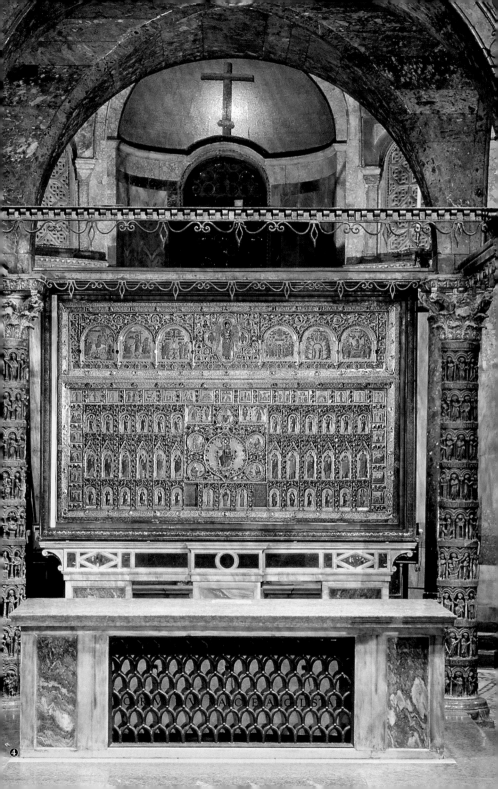

THE CLOCKTOWER

The Clocktower was built at the end of the 15th century to the design of *Mauro Codussi*. Planned as the doorway to the Mercerie (one of the city's main streets), aligned with the Piazzetta and St. Mark's Basin, the tower offers a splendid prospect to those arriving by sea. Above the arch is a large enamelled clockface showing the hours, the moon phases, a sundial and signs of the zodiac; this is topped by a small balcony on which the three Magi pass in procession, and above it are the Moors, the two great bronze figures which still today strike the hours by hammering on the bell.

❶ *The Clocktower in Piazza San Marco.*
❷ *The terrace of the Moors of Venice, so called because of their colour. The two bronze figures represent shepherds who strike the hours by beating a hammer on the bell.*
❸ *Painting by Gabriel Bella of the Conspiracy of Bajomente Tiepolo, with the Clocktower in the background (Fondazione Querini Stampalia).*

THE PROCURATIE

Leaving St. Mark's Basilica, the Procuratie Vecchie, constituting a double loggia in the Venetian-Byzantine style, are to the right. Built in the 12th century under Doge *Sebastiano Ziani* during the Republic to house the apartments of the Procurators of San Marco, they extend for 152 metres with a portico of 50 arches. Partly damaged by fire at the beginning of the 16th century, they were demolished and then rebuilt; the work was completed in 1538, probably with the contribution of *Jacopo Sansovino*.

In front are the Procuratie Nuove, begun by *Scamozzi* at the end of the 16th century and finished by *Longhena* in the 17th century. The style is in harmony with that of the Marciana Library, of which it seems the natural continuation. Napoleon used the buildings for receptions, after which they were reserved for the use of the kings of Italy and today they house the **Museo Correr**, the **Museo del Risorgimento**, the **Museo Archeologico**, the administrative department of the Musei Civici and part of the **Biblioteca Nazionale Marciana**. The 18-century Caffè Florian, the oldest cafe in Italy, is also located here.

❶ *The Napoleonic Wing in the Procuratie.*
❷ *Arcade in the Procuratie.*

The Procuratie were closed in a horseshoe shape after *Napoleon Bonaparte* had the church of San Geminiano razed to the ground (and the extensions of the Procuratie aligned with it) to build what is called the **Napoleonic Wing**. This construction, whose facade on the *piazza* was completed in 1814, was only finished during the Austrian restoration. Since 1922 it has housed the **Museo Correr**, an art gallery and interesting collection of historical relics and documents illustrating the history of Venice. The original nucleus of the museum was established in Palazzo Correr in 1830 as a showcase for Venetian art and history memorabilia collected by the patrician *Teodoro Correr*. Subsequent legacies and acquisitions caused it to be moved first to the Fondaco dei Turchi and then to Piazza San Marco. The museum is organized on two floors: on the first the historical collection and on the second the Museo del Risorgimento and the Quadreria or picture gallery.

❶ *The Procuratie Vecchie.*
❷ *St Mark's Basilica viewed from the Napoleonic Wing in the Procuratie.*
❸ *Piazza San Marco enclosed by the Procuratie, viewed from the Belltower.*

DOGES' PALACE

Residence of the doges, the palace stands where the Grand Canal flows into the lagoon. It was the centre, the heart and the symbol of the Most Serene Republic's power. Nothing remains of the first building, nor of the 12th-century construction. Its current aspect is the result of long and complex reconstructions initiated in the 14th century and coinciding with the systematic reorganization of the surrounding area. The facade of the imposing construction, a splendid example of floral gothic, is decorated with white and rose-coloured geometric designs. It has a double row of arcades in the lower stories (typical of the Venetian *fondaco* palaces), softened by large lancet windows above and crowned by a lace-like parapet of oriental cresting. The palace has an internal courtyard with the spectacular **Giant's Staircase**, designed by *Jacopo Sansovino* in the 16th century, leading to the doges' apartments. The **New Prisons** are connected to the palace by the Bridge of Sighs, whereas the **Piombi** (the Leads) and **Pozzi** (the Wells) are internal prisons.

❶ *Piazzetta di San Marco: the Doges' Palace and in the background the island of San Giorgio.*

❷ *The Porta della Carta connecting St Mark's Basilica to the Doges' Palace.*

❸ *The Doges' Palace viewed from the island of San Giorgio.*

Page 68:
   The Doges' Palace and the Belltower.

Above: Pointed openwork arches in the Doges' Palace.
Below: The Giants' Staircase inside the Doges' Palace.

THE BELL TOWER

The towering bell tower, erected for the first time in the ninth century and rebuilt after it collapsed in 1902 "how it was and where it was", was for centuries the main point of reference for Venetians. Since it was the highest construction in the city it also acted as a lighthouse and look-out tower. Its bells marked the important moments of the Serenissima Republic: the beginning and end of the working day, the meetings of the Maggior Consiglio or Great Council, the assemblies of the senate, and so on. A magnificent panorama of Venice and the lagoon can be enjoyed from the top of the tower, as well as the open sea on one side and the hinterland on the other.

MARCIANA LIBRARY

Jacopo Sansovino's greatest achievement was the Libreria Marciana, the city's main public library, set in front of the Doges' Palace. The building, incomplete at the architect's death, was finished by *Vincenzo Scamozzi* between 1583 and 1588. It was created to house precious Latin and Greek codexes brought from Constantinople in 1453. The facade, with its two orders and Doric arcaded bays interspersed by Ionic columns, has the typical open Venetian loggias and is capped by a terrace and balustrade with three obelisks at the corners and statues of mythological divinities.

❶ *The Libreria Marciana and Piazzetta San Marco.*
❷ *Interior of the Libreria Marciana.*
❸ *The winged lion.*
❹ *St Theodore.*

COLUMNS

In the 13th century two granite columns (from Constantinople) were placed between the Piazzetta and the quay as the monumental access to the marina. The **winged lion**, symbol of St Mark, was placed on top of one column and on the other a statue of **San Theodore,** the first patron of Venice.

❹

②

COFFEE HOUSE

The pavilion, next to the ex royal garden, was designed by *Lorenzo Santi* between 1815 and 1817 and is part of a renewal project promoted by the Napoleonic court. Its neoclassical style is very different from the typical Venice architecture that emphasizes the ornamental aspects of the structure.

BRIDGE OF SIGHS

The Bridge of Sighs was built in 1614 to unite the Doges' Palace with the New Prisons. It consists of two corridors separated by a wall. It is said the that prisoners would sigh at their final view of the sea through the window before being taken down to their cells.

ISLAND OF SAN GIORGIO

This is a typical Venetian island with a monastery consisting of a church, a belltower, an external wall and two lighthouse towers. The buildings are the result of many interventions, including that by *Andrea Palladio*. The island, under Venetian dominion, was donated in 982 to the Benedictine monk *Giovanni Morosini*, who made it the seat of an important Benedictine monastery. Abandoned and left to decay after the fall of the Serenissima Republic, the complex was restored in 1951 when it became the headquarters of the **Giorgio Cini Foundation.**

Above: Aerial view of the island of San Giorgio.

Side: The island of San Giorgio seen from the Doges' Palace.

SAN MOISÈ

Erected, according to records, in the 8th century, the church was reconstructed by *Moisè Valier* who dedicated it to the biblical personage whose name he bore (Moses). It was again restructured In the 12th century after the fire that broke out in the Venice. Instead, the renovation of the interior and the imposing facade date back to the 17th century. Inside there is a late work by *Tintoretto*, **The Washing of the Feet**, and a **Last Supper** attributed to *Palma il Giovane*.

CONTARINI DAL BOVOLO PALACE

Built in the 15th century, the name comes from its spiral staircase, *bovolo* in Venetian. This staircase, not rare in gothic Venice, is set inside a tower with a plethora of pointed arches terminating in an arcade topped by a dome. It is attached to a five-storied loggia.

Side: Santa Maria del Giglio
Below: Details of a statue on the facade

SANTA MARIA DEL GIGLIO

The church of Santa Maria del Giglio, or *Zobenigo*, from the name of the Jubanico family who founded it in the 10th century, has been rebuilt many times until it achieved its current 17th century appearance.

The facade, a baroque masterpiece, was built between 1678 and 1683 by the *Barbaro* family, of which it constitutes an evident self-glorification. Inside, the church has three rectangular chapels on each side and a flat ceiling. In the Molin chapel there is an admirable Madonna and Child with Young St. John, the only painting by *Peter Paul Rubens* preserved in Venice.

LA FENICE THEATRE

Designed in 1790 in the neoclassical style for a society of aristocratic Venetian box holders, La Fenice theatre was inaugurated on 16 May 1792. Rebuilt after a fire in 1836, it became the main Venetian opera house, hosting numerous operatic premieres, included *Giuseppe Verdi's* **La Traviata i**n 1853, soundly booed by the public. Another fire destroyed La Fenice on 29 January 1996, and it did not open again for eight years. Besides being the venue for an important opera season, La Fenice also hosts the **International Festival of Contemporary Music** and, since 2004, the year in which it finally reopened after the latest reconstruction, the **New Year Concert.**

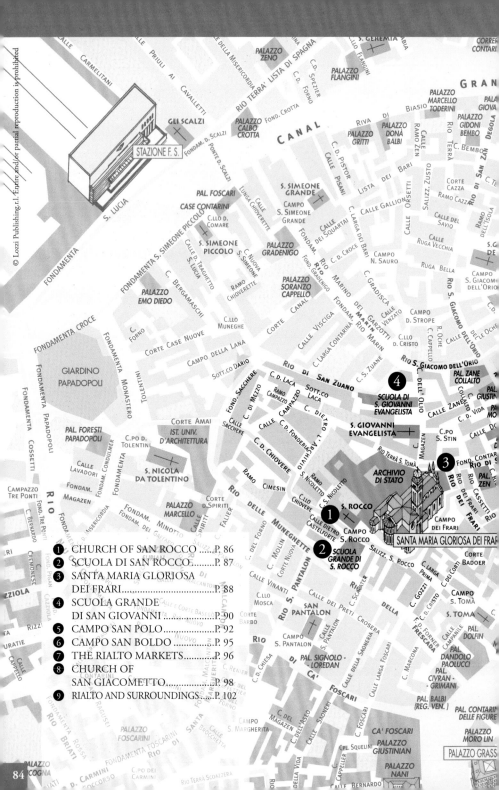

STAZIONE F.S.

GLI SCALZI

S. LUCIA

CANAL

GRAN

PALAZZO ZENO

S. GEREMIA

CORRER CONTARI

PALAZZO FLANGINI

PALAZZO MARCELLO TODERINI

PALAZZO GIOVA

PALAZZO CALBO CROTTA

RIVA DI BIASIO

PALAZZO GRITTI

PALAZZO DONÀ BALBI

PALAZZO GIDONI BEMBO

PAL. FOSCARI

CASE CONTARINI

S. SIMEONE GRANDE

CAMPO S. SIMEONE GRANDE

CORTE CAZZA

C.llo D. COMARE

S. SIMEONE PICCOLO

PALAZZO GRADENIGO

CALLE DEL SAVIO

S.G DE

PALAZZO EMO DIEDO

PALAZZO SORANZO CAPPELLO

CAMPO N. SAURO

RUGA BELLA

CAMPO S. GIACOMO dell'ORIO

GIARDINO PAPADOPOLI

CORTE CASE NUOVE

CAMPO DELLA LANA

CORTE MUNEGHE

CAMPO D. STROPE

R. OCHE

CAMPO DELL'OLIO

RIO DI SAN ZUANE

PALAZZO ZANE COLLALTO

PAL. GIUSTIN

PAL. FORESTI PAPADOPOLI

CORTE AMAI

IST. UNIV. D'ARCHITETTURA

SCUOLA DI S. GIOVANNI EVANGELISTA

S. GIOVANNI EVANGELISTA

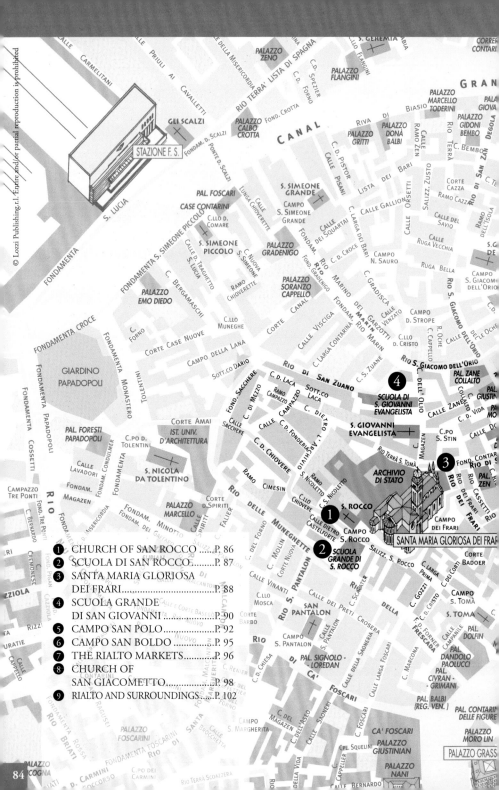 4

S. NICOLA DA TOLENTINO

PALAZZO MARCELLO

CORTE D.SPIRITI

C.po S. STIN

ARCHIVIO DI STATO

RIO TERRÀ S. TOMÀ

3

CAMPAZZO TRE PONTI

S. ROCCO

1

SCUOLA GRANDE DI S. ROCCO

2

CAMPO S. ROCCO

SANTA MARIA GLORIOSA DEI FRARI

CAMPO DEI FRARI

CORTE BADOER

1 CHURCH OF SAN ROCCO .....P. 86
2 SCUOLA DI SAN ROCCO.........P. 87
3 SANTA MARIA GLORIOSA
   DEI FRARI.................P. 88
4 SCUOLA GRANDE
   DI SAN GIOVANNI ....P. 90
5 CAMPO SAN POLO..................P. 92
6 CAMPO SAN BOLDO .....P. 95
7 THE RIALTO MARKETS........P. 96
8 CHURCH OF
   SAN GIACOMETTO................P. 98
9 RIALTO AND SURROUNDINGS.....P. 102

S. TOMA

PAL. DOLFIN

SAN PANTALON

CAMPO S. TOMÀ

PAL. DANDOLO PAOLUCCI

PAL. CIVRAN - GRIMANI

CAMPO S. PANTALON

PAL. SIGNOLO - LOREDAN

CA' FOSCARI

PAL. BALBI (REG. VEN.)

PAL. CONTARINI DELLE FIGURE

PALAZZO FOSCARINI

CAMPO S. MARGHERITA

CA' FOSCARI

PALAZZO GIUSTINIAN

PALAZZO MORO LIN

PALAZZO GRASS

PALAZZO NANI

PALAZZO COGNA

CHURCH OF SAN ROCCO

The church, whose construction in the Renaissance style dates back to 1489, was largely rebuilt in 1725. The same happened to the facade, reconstructed between 1765 and 1771 to a design by *Bernardino Maccaruzzi*. Inside there are several paintings by Tintoretto, including **St. Roch Ministering to Plague Victims, St. Roch Healing the Animals, St. Roch Comforted by an Angel** and **St. Roch Struck by the Plague** in the chancel.

❶ *Interior of the Scuola di San Rocco.*
❷ *The facade of San Rocco.*

SCUOLA GRANDE DI SAN ROCCO

On the paving of campo San Rocco the holes are still visible for the poles of the awning used by the Venetian lords when, after mass on every 16 August - feast day of the protector of plague victims - they entered the Scuola Grande di San Rocco where the confraternity offered a banquet. An evident clue to the importance of this *Scuola*, established immediately after the plague of 1477 and developing over the following decades, is the construction of a great complex, with a church once closely linked to the confraternity, now divided by a footpath created in the 19th century.

❸ *The facade of the Scuola di San Rocco.*
❹ *Canaletto, The Doge Visiting San Rocco, National Gallery, London.*

❸

❹

SANTA MARIA GLORIOSA DEI FRARI

Dedicated to the Assumption of Mary it is one of the most important monuments in Venice, also because of the fine paintings and sculptures it houses. The area occupied by the church and the adjacent ex monastery was donated by Doge *Jacopo Tiepolo* in 1231 to the Minor Franciscan Friars, who built a church there and drained the swamp. The current church was begun around 1330 and finished within the century. It was consecrated in 1492 and dedicated to the Virgin's Assumption into heaven. It is in the classical gothic style with a "Franciscan" influence including a predominance of brickwork without flamboyant elements such as spires, pinnacles and rampant arches. Inside, among the paintings worth seeing there is a magnificent altarpiece depicting the **Assumption** by *Titian* (1518) and the **Ca' Pesaro Madonna** by the same artist, whereas in the sacristy there is the remarkable triptych by *G. Bellini* (1488) of the **Madonna with Child and Four Saints**. There are also numerous sculptures, including **St. John the Baptist** by *Sansovino* (1554) and **St Jerome** by *A. Vittoria* (1564). On 12 May 1810, the religious community of the friars was dissolved and the building become a parish church.

Titian, The Assumption

SCUOLA GRANDE DI SAN GIOVANNI

Founded in 1261, it is one of the Serenissima Republic's richest and most prestigious *scuole*. In the 15th century, it had become important within the Venetian community and between 1414-1420 it was renovated and gradually enriched with notable art works. After the confraternity was dissolved in 1806, the building was stripped of most of its works. The complex is entered from the gateway to the courtyard. Inside, the vast hall on the ground floor is divided Into two aisles by columns with gothic capitols. The magnificent Renaissance staircase by *Mauro Codussi* leads to a large upper room, the *salone* of St John or **Chapterhouse,** a masterpiece by *Giorgio Massari*. On the far wall is the altar dedicated to the saint, with his statue in the centre. From this room you enter the **Oratory of the Cross**, where a piece of the True Cross has been kept since it was donated to the confraternity in1369 by the chancellor of the kingdom of Cyprus. The **Sala dell'Albergo** preserves its 16th-century layout and is decorated with four large canvases by *Palma il Giovane*.

Side: Renaissance doorway crowned by the eagle symbol of the evangelist
Above: The sumptuous polychrome marble floor in the Sala Capitolare

❶

❶ The facade of the two
Soranzo palaces in campo
San Polo: "casa vecchia"
(left) and "casa nuova"
The facades, now united by
the same colour of plaster
and by the windows on
the ground floor, have
medieval, gothic and 15th-
century elements
❷ Campo San Polo.
❸ Church of San Polo.

❷

CAMPO SAN POLO

The Campo San Polo is the largest *campo* in Venice. There used to be a market here, as well as archery and crossbow contests and, above all, bullfights. The **Palazzo Soranzo** and the church of **San Polo** overlook the *campo*.

❸

Above:
    Palazzo Corner Mocenigo from the side facing Campo San Polo
Side:
    The Bridge and Fondamenta delle Tette, or of the Tits, named after a
    famous brothel in this area

CAMPO SAN BOLDO

Here you can see the *masegni*, the stone used to pave the *calli* and *campi* of Venice made of trachyte, a stone of volcanic origin extracted from mines in the Euganean Hills. These stones, 30 to 40 centimetres wide and of various lengths, were used to pave Venice as early as the first half of the 18th century. The ancient *masegni* were 25 centimetres thick, whereas the current ones are much thinner.

THE RIALTO MARKETS

The Rialto area has been famous for its markets since 1097. A lively meeting place for Venetians and foreigners and an opportunity for business and cultural exchanges, furnished over the centuries with warehouses, shops, inns and eating places. Fish, fruit and vegetables are still today sold in the Rialto markets, always crowded with both locals and tourists. The heart of the markets is the **Campo San Giacomo.**

Most of the fish stalls are to be found under the arcades of the Pescheria, in the *campo* of the same name, overlooked by the **statue** of **St. Peter,** "fisher of souls". The catch mainly comes from the Tonchetto market, with a wide variety of fish, molluscs and shellfish from the lagoon and the Adriatic sea. The fruit and vegetable market, the **Erberia**, offers seasonal produce at good prices. It is also worth making a detour to the **Antica Drogheria Mascari**, the oldest in Venice, striking for the colourful spices on show in its windows.

CHURCH OF ST GIACOMETTO

In the Campo San Giacomo in Rialto, at the time of the Republic the centre of commercial and financial business and where there is still a market today, is the church of San Giacometto. It is believed to be the oldest church in Venice, supposedly founded at the beginning of the 5th century, together with the city. Rebuilt in the 12th century, it miraculously survived the fire of 1514. A relic of the older building is the portico with wooden architrave on the exterior, supported by five columns with Gothic capitals, an element often to be found in the early Venetian churches. The Greek- cross interior is inserted in a square with a central dome and enriched with medieval columns and capitals. The other sides of the *campo* are occupied by the **Fabbriche Vecchie** and by the portico of the **Banco Giro**, under which the bankers set out their tables for the merchants' payments. In front of the church there is the 16th-century statue of the **Hunchback of Rialto,** a kneeling figure supporting the staircase leading to the **Colonna del Bando**, from where the *comandador* announced the laws and judgements of the Republic.

❶ ❷ *The Church of San Giacometto with its ancient bell gable, clock and gothic arcade.*

❸ *Canaletto, St James at Rialto, Gemäldegalerie, Dresden.*

❹ *The Rialto hunchback.*

Next page:
The Rialto Bridge

LAPIS · LEGIBVS · REIP
EDICENDIS
AERE · CIVICO · RESTITVTVS
A · MDCCCXXXVI

RIALTO
AND SURROUNDINGS

The village of *Rivoaltus*, built on the banks of the Rio Businiacus – the future Grand Canal – was the first Venetian "district" and is still today one of the most characteristic and lively areas of the city. This vivacity came from the establishment of a new general market in 1097 on the Rialtine islands. Over the years this became the authentic heart of the Republic's business. Besides the commercial activities, with the wholesale and retail markets and the jewellers' shops, this was also the centre of financial life, with commodity exchanges and maritime insurance agencies, as well as the major Venetian magistrates linked to trade. It was these activities that

①

②

helped the Rialto district to achieve its particular urban conformation, thanks also to its original characteristics, so different from the rest of Venice. The presence of long *calli* alternating with short *calli* and *campi*, the connections between the areas and the total absence of bridges enabled a faster movement of people and goods. Unfortunately almost all the ancient buildings in the area were destroyed by a fire in 1514. The rebuilding by Antonio Abbondi, or *Scarpagnino*, greatly altered the image of the Rialto with new constructions such as the **Fabbriche Vecchie** and **Nuove** and the **Palazzo dei Camerlenghi**. However its particular layout remained more or less unchanged.

❶ *Gondolas alongside the Rialto Bridge.*
❷ *View of the Grand Canal from Rialto.*
❸ *Venetian window with directions.*
❹ *Campo San Bartolomeo.*
❺ *Palazzo Centani, where Goldoni lived.*

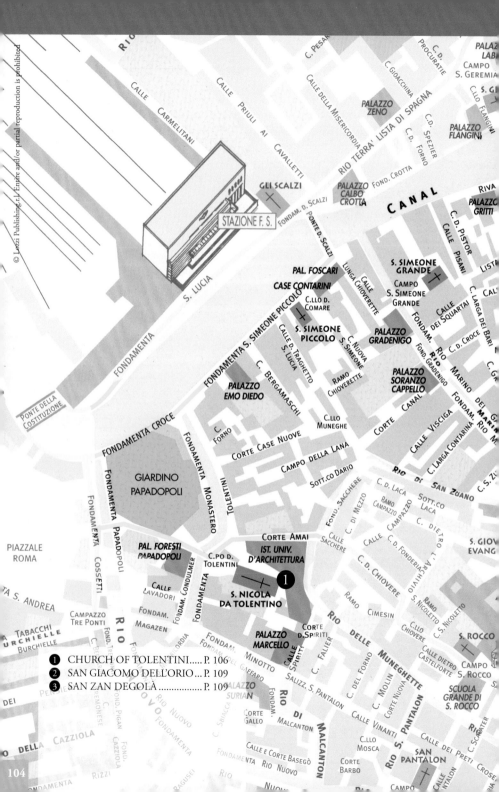

RIO

CALLE CARMELITANI

CALLE PRIULI AI CAVALLETTI

CALLE DELLA MISERICORDIA

C. PESARO

CALLE DELLA MISERICORDIA

C. GIOACCHINA

C. D. PROCURATIE

PALAZZO LAB

CAMPO S. GEREMIA

S. GE

PALAZZO ZENO

RIO TERRA LISTA DI SPAGNA

C. D. SPEZIER

C. D. FORNO

PALAZZO FLANGINI

C.llo FLANGINI

GLI SCALZI

STAZIONE F. S.

S. LUCIA

FONDAM. D. SCALZI

PONTE D. SCALZI

FONDAM. D. SCALZI

PALAZZO CALBO CROTTA

Fond. CROTTA

CANAL

RIVA

PALAZZO GRITTI

C. D. PISTOR

CALLE PISANI

PAL. FOSCARI

CASE CONTARINI

CALLE LUNGA CHIOVERETTE

S. SIMEONE GRANDE

LISTA

FONDAMENTA S. SIMEONE PICCOLO

C.llo D. COMARE

CALLE CHIOVERETTE

Campo S. Simeone Grande

CALLE DEI SQUARTAI

C. LARGA DEI BARI

S. SIMEONE PICCOLO

CALLE D. TRAGHETTO

S. LUCIA

C. NUOVA

S. SIMEONE

PALAZZO GRADENIGO

FONDAM. RIO

FOND. GRADENIGO

C. D. CROCE

PONTE DELLA COSTITUZIONE

FONDAMENTA

C. BERGAMASCHI

RAMO CHIOVERETTE

PALAZZO SORANZO CAPPELLO

FONDAM. RIO MARINO

C. DEI MARIN

C. G

PALAZZO EMO DIEDO

C. FORNO

C.llo MUNEGHE

CORTE CANAL

CALLE VISCIGA

C. LARGA CONTARINA

FONDAMENTA CROCE

FONDAMENTA MONASTERO

CORTE CASE NUOVE

CAMPO DELLA LANA

SOTT.CO DARIO

RIO DI SAN ZUANO

C. S. ZU

FONDAMENTA PAPADOPOLI

GIARDINO PAPADOPOLI

TOLENTINI

FONU. SACCHERE

C. D. LACA

C. DI MEZZO

RAMO CAMPAZZO

SOTT.CO LACA

C. DIETRO

S. GIOV EVANG

FONDAMENTA PAPADOPOLI

COSSETTI

PAL. FORESTI PAPADOPOLI

FONDAM. CONDULMER

FONDAMENTA

CORTE AMAI

IST. UNIV. D'ARCHITETTURA

CALLE SACCHERE

CALLE C. D. FONDERIA

C. D. CHIOVERE

RAMO

S. NICOLETTO

S. NICOLETTO

C.llo CHIOVERE

PIAZZALE ROMA

CALLE LAVADORI

C.PO D. TOLENTINI

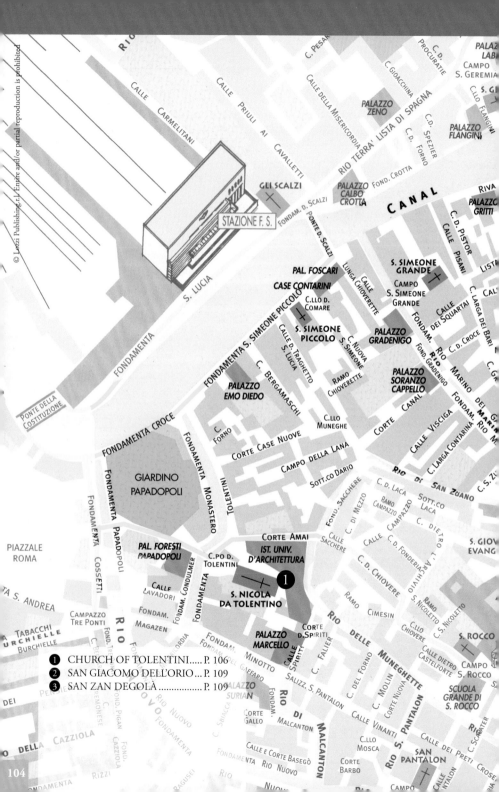 1

S. NICOLA DA TOLENTINO

CIMESIN

RAMO

S. ROCCO

TA S. ANDREA

TABACCHI URCHIELLE

CAMPAZZO TRE PONTI

FONDAM. MAGAZEN

FONDAM.

PALAZZO MARCELLO

CORTE D.SPIRITI

RIO DELLE MUNEGHETTE

CALLE DIETRO CASTELFORTE

S. ROCCO

Campo S. ROCCO

SCUOLA GRANDE DI S. ROCCO

Burchielle

MINOTTO

CALLE SPIRITI

FALIER

C. DEL FORNO

CALLE VINANTI

RIO S. PANTALON

RIO NUOVO

FONDAM. GAFFARO

SALIZZ. S. PANTALON

CORTE NUOVA

CALLE DEI PRETI

SAN PANTALON

DEI

PALAZZO SURIAN

CORTE GALLO

FONDAM. MALCANTON

C. MOLIN

RIO DI MALCANTON

C. SBIACCA

CAZZIOLA

FONDAMENTA RIO NUOVO

CALLE E CORTE BASEGÒ

CORTE BARBO

C.llo MOSCA

CAMPO

RIZZI

1 CHURCH OF TOLENTINI.....P. 106
2 SAN GIACOMO DELL'ORIO...P. 109
3 SAN ZAN DEGOLÀ.................P. 109

CHURCH OF TOLENTINI

The 18th-century facade of the church of San Nicolò dei Tolentini, known as the Tolentini church, was designed by *Andrea Tirali* in the classical style whereas the interior is by *Scamozzi*. Inside there is the funerary monument of the bishop *Francesco Morosini*.

Campiello delle Stroppe with its central well.

SAN GIACOMO DELL'ORIO

Built in the 11th century it has undergone a series of renovations and is now a mixture of different styles. It seems to have taken its name from the swamp on which it stood.

SAN ZAN DEGOLÀ

The church of St. John Decollate was built in 1007 by the *Venier* family. It is one of the oldest In Venice and contains interesting frescoes discovered during its restoration, completed in 1994.

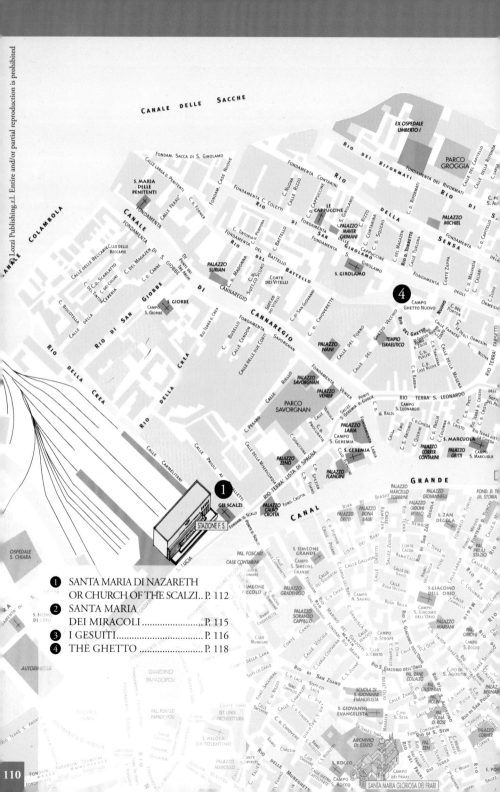

CANALE DELLE SACCHE

EX OSPEDALE
UMBERTO I

PARCO
GROGGIA

RIO DEI RIFORMATI

Fondamenta dei Riformati

PALAZZO
MICHIEL

Fondam. Sacca di S. Girolamo

S. MARIA
DELLE
PENITENTI

Fondamenta Contarini

RIO

DELLA

SENSA

Fondamenta

Calle Larga D. Penitenti

Calle Ferau

C. D. Forner

Fondam. Case Nuove

Fondamenta C. Coletti

LE
CAPPUCCINE

PALAZZO
MAVER
GRIMANI

RIO D. TORRETTE

Calle Turloni

Corte Zappa

Fondamenta

COLAMBOLA

CANALE

COLAMBOLA

FONDAMENTA

Calle delle Beccarie
Beccaria

C. D. Scarlatto

C. dei Colori

C. del Tintor

C. D. Madonna

PALAZZO
SURIAN

Corte
DEI VITELLI

S. GIROLAMO

Campo
S. Giobbe

RIO DI SAN

GIOBBE

CANNAREGIO

Fondamenta

CANNAREGIO

RIO

DELLA

CREA

C. D. CHIOVERETTE

PALAZZO
NANI

TEMPIO
ISRAELITICO

4

Campo
GHETTO NUOVO

RIO

DEL

GHETTO

Ghetto Vecchio

PALAZZO
SAVORGNAN

PALAZZO
VENIER

PARCO
SAVORGNAN

RIO TERRA S. LEONARDO

Campo
S. LEONARDO

S. MARCUOLA

PALAZZO
LABIA

Campo
S. Geremia

S. GEREMIA

PALAZZO
CORRER
CONTARINI

PALAZZO
GRITTI

S. Marcuola

PALAZZO
ZENO

RIO TERRA LISTA DI SPAGNA

PALAZZO
CALBO
CROTTA

PALAZZO
FLANGINI

GRANDE

1

GLI SCALZI

STAZIONE F. S.

PALAZZO
GRITTI

RIVA
DI
BIASIO

CANAL

S. LUCIA

OSPEDALE
S. CHIARA

PAL. FOSCARI

CASE CONTARINI

S. SIMEONE
GRANDE

S. SIMEONE
PICCOLO

PALAZZO
GRADENIGO

PALAZZO
SORANZO
CAPPELLO

S. GIACOMO
DELL'ORIO

AUTORIMESSA

GIARDINO
PAPADOPOLI

S. NICOLA
DA TOLENTINO

SCUOLA DI
S. GIOVANNI
EVANGELISTA

S. GIOVANNI
EVANGELISTA

ARCHIVIO
DI STATO

S. ROCCO

SANTA MARIA GLORIOSA DEI FRARI

1 SANTA MARIA DI NAZARETH
OR CHURCH OF THE SCALZI.. P. 112
2 SANTA MARIA
DEI MIRACOLI .... P. 115
3 I GESUITI .... P. 116
4 THE GHETTO .... P. 118

5
CANNAREGIO

OSPEDALE
FATEBENEFRATELLI

DEGLI ZECCHINI
C. GRADISCA
Calle Larga Piave
C.LLO PIAVE

MADONNA DELL'ORTO

Fondam. Madonna dell'Orto

PALAZZO
LOREDAN
PALAZZO
ARDIGO
Fondamenta
RIO MADONNA
RIO
DELL' ORTO
DELLA
PALAZZO
S. MARCILLA

CASINO DEGLI
SPIRITI

PALAZZO
CONTARINI DAL ZAFFO

SACCA DELLA
MISERICORDIA

C. D'Antona
C.llo
Foscari

CANALE

DELLE

Corte D. Muti

Corte Vecchia

SCUOLA VECCHIA
D. MISERICORDIA
S. MARIA
D. MISERICORDIA

Calle Larga

Calle Lunga

Calle Massena

EX CONVENTO
S. M. DEI SERVI
CAPPELLA DEL
VOLTO SANTO

Fondam. Moro

SCUOLA NUOVA
D. MISERICORDIA

CANALE DELLA MISERICORDIA

EX CHIESA DI
SANTA CATERINA

C. M. FOSCARINI

FONDAMENTA

NUOVE

GESUITI

PALAZZO
ZEN

PALAZZO
DONA

FONDAMENTA

PALAZZO
DIEDO
SAN
MARZIALE
RIO DE
SERVI

MISERICORDIA
Fondam.
della

PALAZZO
LEZZE

CAMPO
S. ANTONIO

CONVENTO
Fond. Gesuiti

RAMO
DONA

③

S. FOSCA
LA
MADDALENA
PALAZZO
CORNER
CONTARINI
PALAZZO
SORANZO
PALAZZO
EMO

RIO DELLA MADDALENA

NOALE

PALAZZO
VENDRAMIN

SCUOLA NUOVA
D. MISERICORDIA

PALAZZO
PAPAFAVA

RIO DI

CAMPO
S. ANTONIO

CATERINA

DEI

CONVENTO
Fond. Gesuiti

Calle
Larga dei
Botteri

Fondamenta

S. FOSCA
Corte
Barbaro

PALAZZO
GIOVANELLI

S. FELICE

CALLE DELLA RACCHETTA

Corte
Squero
Vecchio

SANTA

FONDAMENTA

NUOVE

RIO DI SANTA

Fond. S. Andrea

DOLCE

Fond. D. Sartori

CATERINA

Calle
Larga

DEI

Corte
Carità

C.llo
di Pietà

PANADA

Corte
del Paludo

C.llo
Widman

RIO

DELLA
C.llo
d. Cason

S. SOFIA

RIO DI CA' SOFIA

CAMPO
S. STAE

CA' PESARO
(GALL. D'ARTE MODER.)
PALAZZO
DONA
PAL CORNER
D. REGINA

CA' D'ORO

STRADA

CAMPO
S. SOFIA

CASA
FAVRETTO PALAZZO
BRANDOLIN

CANAL

NUOVA

SS. APOSTOLI

CAMPO DEI
SS. APOSTOLI

RIO DEI
SANTI

S. CANCIANO

APOSTOLI

PALAZZO
WIDMAN

C.llo
WIDMAN

PAL.
MORO

S. CASSIANO
S. CASSIANO
PALAZZO
MUTI BAGLIONI

PALAZZO
GOZZI

CAMPO
BECCARIE

C.po DELLA
PESCARIA

PESCARIA

FABBRICHE
NUOVE

RIO SAN

Salizz. SS. APOSTOLI

CAMPO
S. MARIA
NOVA

S. GIOVANNI
CRISOSTOMO

PAL. BEMBO
E BOLDU

S. MARIA DEI MIRACOLI

PALAZZO
SORANZO
VAN AXEL

SS. GIOVANNI E PAOLO

GRANDE

FABBRICHE
VECCHIE

S. GIOVANNI
ELEMOSINARIO

CAMPO DI
RIALTO
NUOVO

S. GIOVANNI
CRISOSTOMO

TEATRO
MALIBRAN

②

RIO DI SAN MARINA

CAMPO
S. MARINA

PAL.
PISANI

PALAZZO
DONA

PALAZZO
CAMERLENGHI

FONDACO
DEI TEDESCHI

PALAZZO
MOLIN
CAPPELLO

S. APONAL

PONTE DI RIALTO

RIO FONTEGO

SCALETTA

SALIZZADA

FAVA

PALAZZO
RUZZINI

PALAZZO
PADOPOLI

S. SILVESTRO

SAN
BARTOLOMEO

S. LIO

CAMPO
S. LIO

CAMPO
S. MARIA
FORMOSA

PALAZZO
RAVA

PALAZZO
MANIN

1 • THE GRAND CANAL
P. 12

2 • SAN MARCO
P. 44

3 • SAN POLO
P. 84

4 • SANTA CROCE
P. 104

6 • DORSODURO
AND GIUDECCA
P. 120

7 • CASTELLO
P. 134

8 • ISLANDS
P. 146

SCUOLA G.
DI SAN M.

SS. GIOVANNI E PAOLO

111

SANTA MARIA DI NAZARETH OR CHURCH OF THE SCALZI

Longhena was commissioned to build the church, overlooking the Grand Canal, in 1654. *Giuseppe Pozzo* is responsible for the interior decoration and *Giuseppe Sardi* for the facade, divided into two orders in Carrara marble with columns framing the entrance and the niches. It has one aisle with side chapels, illuminated by large windows.

Above:
  Santa Maria of Nazareth, called of the Scalzi
Below: The Ponte delle Guglie

❶ *Campiello del Remer with a characteristic well. A craftsman who built oars for Venetian vessels used to work here.*

❷ *Corte del Milion, recalling the Italian name for the Travels of Marco Polo.*

❸ *Marco Polo (1254-1324), Venetian merchant and one of the greatest explorers of all times. Together with his father Niccolò and uncle Matteo, he was one of the first to arrive in China along the Silk Road.*

Above:
  Palazzo Soranzo Van Axel overlooking the Canale della Panada.

Side:
  The internal courtyard of Palazzo Soranzo Van Axel with its open stairway, arcade and well.

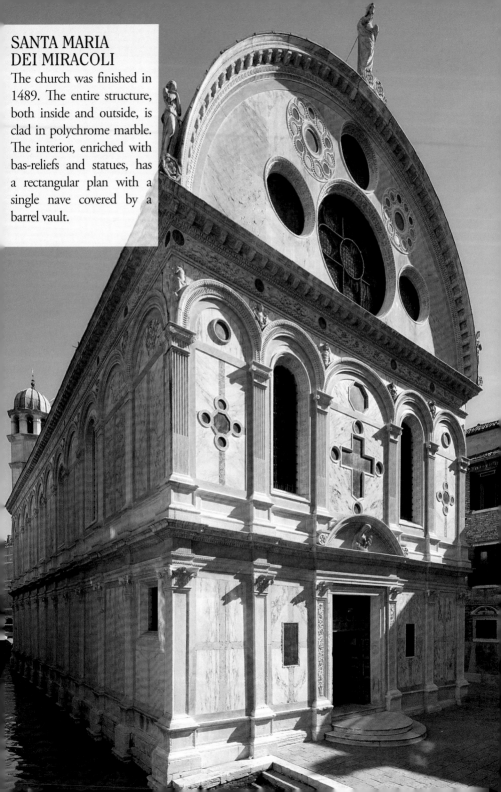

SANTA MARIA DEI MIRACOLI

The church was finished in 1489. The entire structure, both inside and outside, is clad in polychrome marble. The interior, enriched with bas-reliefs and statues, has a rectangular plan with a single nave covered by a barrel vault.

❶ ❷

I GESUITI

The Jesuits had the church of the Assumption of Mary built in the 19th century in place of the previous one, to stress their triumphant return to the city after they had been banished. The high facade is in the Venetian baroque style, and the interior is striking for its magnificent marble decoration. There is an impressive **Martyrdom of St. Lawrence** by *Titian* on the first altar to the left, undoubtedly one of the most evocative nocturnes in the history of art.

❸

❶ *The church of the Jesuits.*
❷ *San Alvise with its gabled brick facade, typical of the 14th century.*
❸ *The Chiesa della Madonna dell'Orto.*

THE GHETTO

The word ghetto was coined precisely in Venice, indicating the foundries located in the area (*geto* in dialect), where the Venetian Jews were obliged to live during the Republic period. The ghetto is still centre of Jewish life in the city. They are two synagogues in use and almost all the community buildings still have institutional functions.

❶ *Campo del Ghetto Novo*
❷ *The interior of a synagogue.*
❸ *The bridge with three arches.*
❹ *Bridges in the Ghetto.*

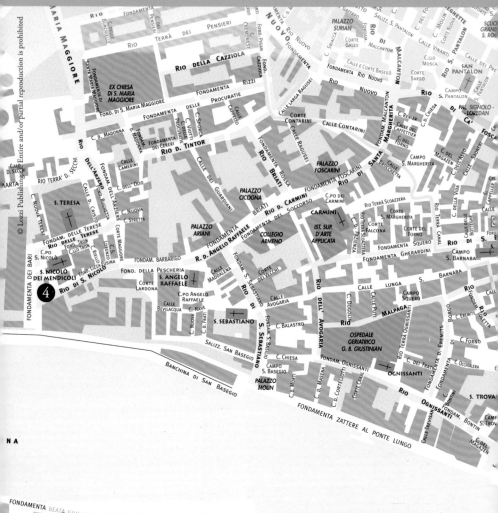

1. THE CHURCH TO OUR LADY
   OF HEALTH OR SALVATION... P. 122
2. PALAZZO VENIER DEI LEONI
   (GUGGENHEIM MUSEUM) .. P. 126
3. THE ACCADEMIA
   MUSEUM GALLERY .... P. 128
4. SAN NICOLÒ
   DEI MENDICOLI .... P. 133

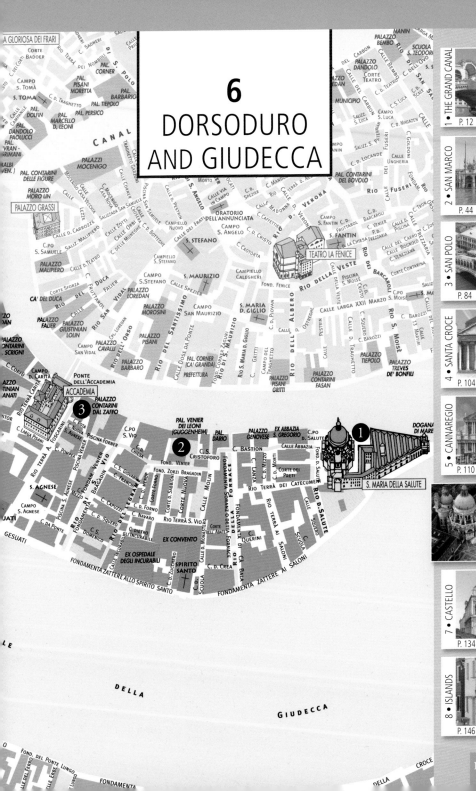

A GLORIOSA DEI FRARI

6
DORSODURO
AND GIUDECCA

TEATRO LA FENICE

PALAZZO GRASSI

ACCADEMIA

PONTE DELL'ACCADEMIA

PALAZZO CONTARINI DAL ZAFFO

PAL. VENIER DEI LEONI (GUGGENHEIM)

S. MARIA DELLA SALUTE

DELLA

GIUDECCA

1 • THE GRAND CANAL
P. 12

2 • SAN MARCO
P. 44

3 • SAN POLO
P. 84

4 • SANTA CROCE
P. 104

5 • CANNAREGIO
P. 110

7 • CASTELLO
P. 134

8 • ISLANDS
P. 146

THE CHURCH TO OUR LADY OF HEALTH OR SALVATION

The church to Our Lady of Health or Salvation was the result of a solemn vow taken by Doge *Nicolò Contarini* after the terrible plague of 1630; the building works, entrusted to *Longhena*, lasted fifty years and were completed In 1687. Built in Istrian stone, the church is set on a high platform reached by a ceremonial flight of steps. The impressive facade shows the influence of Palladian classicism and is scanned by six chapels. The great semi-spherical dome surrounded by statues crowns the building. Inside, the walls define the space separated by robust arches and pillars in grey stone supporting the drum of the dome and dividing the great central nave from the ambulatory, surrounded by the chapels linked with the sacristy by internal corridors. The church contains precious works of art such as the admirable **Pentecost** and other paintings by *Titian,* **The Marriage at Cana by** *Tintoretto* **and Jonah and Samson** by *Palma il Giovane.*

Opposite page:
Interior of Santa
Maria della
Salute.

On this page:
❶ Detail of marble
floor.
❷ The great dome.

❶

❷

PALAZZO VENIER DEI LEONI (GUGGENHEIM MUSEUM)

Construction on Palazzo Venier dei Leoni was begun in 1749 for the powerful *Venier* family. Work stopped after the first story was built and it was never finished. Later bought by the rich and eccentric art collector *Peggy Guggenheim*, it became a museum of modern art as well as her home until her death in 1979. The palace is now owned by the **Solomon R. Guggenheim Foundation** of New York and is open exclusively as a museum.

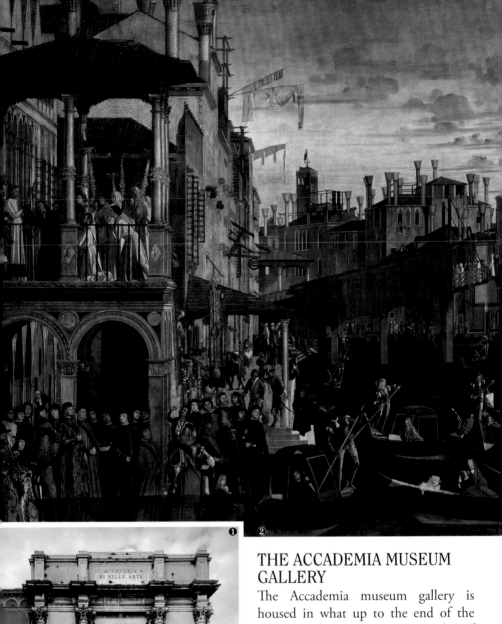

❶ ❷

THE ACCADEMIA MUSEUM GALLERY

The Accademia museum gallery is housed in what up to the end of the 19th century was the vast complex of the church of Santa Maria della Carità, the convent of the Canonici Lateranensi and the Scuola Grande of Santa Maria della Carità. It is now a magnificent museum housing masterpieces of Venetian

and Veneto art, with particular reference to the period between the 15th and 18th centuries. It contains works by *Giorgione*, *Giovanni Bellini*, *Vittore Carpaccio*, *Tintoretto* and *Titian*, among others. Also exhibited here, although only on special occasions, is *Leonardo da Vinci's* famous drawing of **Vitruvian Man**.

❶ *The main entrance of the Gallerie dell'Accademia.*

❷ *Vittore Carpaccio, Miracle of the Relic of the Holy Cross at the Rialto bridge.*

❸ *Giovanni Mansueti, Miraculous Cure of the Daughter of Benvegnudo da San Polo.*

❶ *Vittore Carpaccio,*
Arrival of the
Ambassadors.
❷ *Paolo Veronese, The*
Feast in the House of
Levi.
❸ *Giorgione, The*
Tempest.

❶ *Ca' Zenobio or Armenian Boys' School.*
❷ *View from the Fondamenta delle Zattere overlooking the Giudecca canal.*
❸ *San Trovaso, where Palladio's influence is clear to see.*
❹ *Santa Maria del Rosario, called of the Gesuati, begun in 1715 and completed by Giorgio Massari in the Palladian style.*

SAN NICOLÒ DEI MENDICOLI

St. Nicholas of the Beggars, albeit having undergone partial reconstructions over the centuries, is one of the few churches in Venice to have preserved its 13th century Veneto-Byzantine style. The facade, with Its great central rose window topped by a small 13th-century double lancet window, has a portico (partly rebuilt with the original materials) often found on old churches to offer shelter to the poor. The interior dates back to the 13th-15th centuries, has a basilica-type plan with a nave and two aisles divided by squat columns with 14th-century capitals. The transept has two pointed arches dating from the 15th century. It houses a fine painting of **The Resurrection by** *Palma il Giovane.*

1 SCUOLA DI SAN MARCO
AND CHURCH OF SANTI
GIOVANNI AND PAOLO .... P. 136
2 PALAZZO QUERINI
STAMPALIA .... P. 141
3 CHURCH OF PIETÀ.............. P. 142
4 SAN ZACCARIA .... P. 142
5 THE ARSENAL .... P. 144

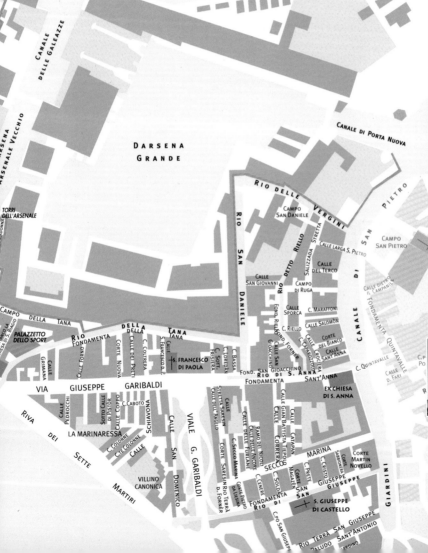

7
CASTELLO

1 • THE GRAND CANAL
P. 12

2 • SAN MARCO
P. 44

3 • SAN POLO
P. 84

4 • SANTA CROCE
P. 104

5 • CANNAREGIO
P. 110

6 • DORSODURO AND GIUDECCA
P. 120

9 • FARI
P. Po

8 • ISLANDS
P. 146

CANALE DELLE GALEAZZE

DARSENA ARSENALE VECCHIO

TORRI DELL'ARSENALE

CANALE DI PORTA NUOVA

DARSENA GRANDE

RIO DELLE VERGINI

CAMPO SAN DANIELE

PIETRO

RIO DETTO RIELLO STRETTA

SALIZZADA

CALLE LARGA S. PIETRO

CAMPO SAN PIETRO

RIO SAN DANIELE

CALLE DEL TERCO

CALLE DIETRO IL CAMPANILE

CALLE San Giovanni

CAMPO DI RUGA

CANALE DI SAN

FONDAMENTA QUINTAVALLE

CALLE Sporca

C. MARATTONI

C. RIELLO

FOND. RIELLO FORNER

CALLE SALOMON

CALLE San GIOACCHINO

CORTE DEL BIANCO

C. CAVAZOCCA

CORTE CAVAZOCCA

CALLE SANT'ANNA

C. QUINTAVALLE

CALLE 9. FARI

CAMPO DELLA TANA

RIO FONDAMENTA DELLA TANA

DELLA TANA

CHIESA DI S. BIAGIO

MADONNA

PALAZZETTO DELLO SPORT

CALLE GRIMANA

CALLE FORNI

CALLE CAPPO

CORTE NUOVA

C. CORBERA

S. FRANCESCO D.P.

C. COREDAN

C. SOTT. PISTOR

C. BASSA

S. FRANCESCO DI PAOLA

FOND. SAN GIOACCHINO

RIO DI S. ANNA

Fondamenta

SANT'ANNA

EX CHIESA DI S. ANNA

RIVA DEI SETTE MARTIRI

VIA GIUSEPPE GARIBALDI

CALLE PEDROCCHI

SOTTO CALLE DI PISTOR

C. CABOTO

C. LE COLONNE

C. TE COLONNE

CALLE

LA MARINARESSA

SCHIAVONA

VIALE G. GARIBALDI

CALLE SAN DOMENICO

VILLINO CANONICA

CALLE DELL'ANGLO

STRETTA SARESIN

CALLE DELL'ANGLO

RAMO DEL NICOLI

C. LE DELLE INCORE

CORTE SARESIN

C. SEGGIO MARINA

CORTE SARESIN RIO TERRÀ D. FORNER

CALLE GIAN BATTISTA TIEPOLO

CALLE CATAPAN

CALLE CORRERA

MARINA

SECCO

C. PRETE

C. DELLE FURLANE

CALLE PIETRO DA LESINA

C. CERERE

C. MAGAZEN

C. SOLDANA

FONDAMENTA

RIO DI SAN

SAN CRISTO

C. PELE

C. CERESTO

GIUSEPPE

CORTE MARTIN NOVELLO

S. GIUSEPPE DI CASTELLO

RIO TERRA SAN GIUSEPPE

RIO TERRA SAN GIUSEPPE

PALUDO

SANT'ANTONIO

GIARDINI

SCUOLA DI SAN MARCO AND
CHURCH OF SANTI GIOVANNI AND PAOLO

Initiated in 1246 on land donated by Doge *Jacopo Tiepolo* to the Dominican friars, the church was completed during the 14th century in the Gothic style on the plan of the conventual basilica with a Latin cross layout. It is the largest Gothic church in Venice. The brick facade, divided into three by two pilasters, is balanced by a succession, in the lower order, of deep, pointed niches. The marble doorway combines Gothic and Renaissance elements and is framed by

coupled columns. Inside, the imposing central nave has a cross vault ceiling supported by columns that, united by the wooden beams, divide the pointed arches. The church contains paintings by *Giovanni Bellini, Lorenzo Lotto, Cima da Conegliano* and *Paolo Veronese*.

Adjoining the church is the Renaissance building of the **Scuola Grande di San Marco**. In 1807, under Napoleonic domination, it became a military hospital and then a civil hospital, still in use today.

Previous page:
  Scuola Grande di San Marco.
This page:
❶ *Church of SS Giovanni e Paolo.*
❷ *Equestrian statue of the famous condottiere Bartolomeo Colleoni, made in 1479.*
❸ *Corte Botera. It takes its name from the trade of the botteri (barrel makers) who worked here.*
❹ *San Francesco della Vigna.*

Above: Interior garden of Palazzo Querini Stampalia.
Below: Palazzo Priuli Ruzzini, overlooking Campo Santa Maria Formosa.

PALAZZO QUERINI STAMPALIA

The palace dates back to the early 16th century. Since 1869 it has housed the foundation of the same name, set up by the last descendent of the family, Count *Giovanni Querini Stampalia*. There is a **Library** on the first floor with over 300,000 volumes including manuscripts, incunabula, ancient and modern books. The **Art Gallery** is on the second floor, a notable collection of 400 paintings of the Venetian, Italian and foreign schools.

Above: Palazzo Querini Stampalia housing the foundation of the same name
Below: Santa Maria Formosa. Founded in the 7th century and amply reconstructed,
it was designed in its present form in 1492 by Mauro Codussi

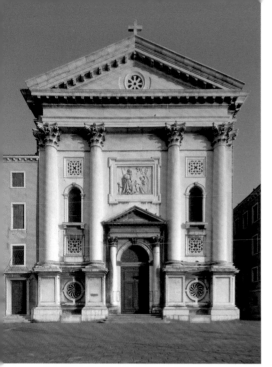

CHURCH OF PIETÀ

The church, built between 1745 and 1760 and designed by *Giorgio Massari*, belongs to the orphanage of the same name. Like the other *"ospedali maggiori"* of the city it was famous for the musical performances of the orphans under the direction of famous *maestri* (including *Antonio Vivaldi*). The facade in Istrian stone was completed in 1906. The interior, with an atrium insulating it from external noise, is an elegant hall designed for musical events, with its characteristic rounded corners, the absence of chapels and large choirs on the entrance and side walls.

Side: Palazzo Dandolo, now Hotel Danieli

SAN ZACCARIA

The Benedictine monastery of San Zaccaria is a vast complex set around two colonnaded cloisters. The round arches of the 15th-century portico form the entrance to the ancient cemetery, whereas the brick facade of the original church can be seen on the right. The interior has a nave and two aisles. Wide round arches are supported by sturdy columns resting on high octagonal plinths with "ancient style" capitals bearing spread eagles. Notable paintings include the **Holy Conversation** by *Bellini* and **Birth of John the Baptist** by *Tintoretto*.

THE ARSENAL

Cited in Dante's *Inferno*, the construction of the Arsenal began in the 13th century. It is a vast (45 ha or 110 acres) and complex monument of great historical importance. The oldest nucleus consists of two rows of naval shipyards (*squeri*) alonside the **Darsena Vecchia or Old Dock**. Access is from St. Mark's Basin through the main entrance with its two impressive crenulated towers. The other entrance, the **Porta di Terra** or **Land Gateway**, also called **Lion's Gateway**, was instead built in the 17th century around Roman triumphal archways. The shipyards were operational until the early 20th century, when the complex started to fall into decay, only partly compensated by the presence, in the Corderie area, of the **Venice Biennale**.

However a project is being studied for its general reconversion and restoration.

❸

❻

❶ *The Biennale gardens.*
❷ ❸ *The imposing entrance to the Arsenal.*
❹ ❺ *The Venice Biennale.*
❻ *View of the Arsenal Gaggiandre, built in 1568-1573 perhaps to a design by Jacopo Sansovino.*

Islands

MURANO BURANO TORCELLO LIDO

MURANO

The name probably comes from Am-
murianum, the name of a gate in
Altinum, the city of origin of the refugees who, driven out by the barbarian invasions, arrived on this island
in the early Middle Ages. The international fame of Murano, an autonomous municipality from the end of
the 13th century up to 1923 when it
became part of Venice, is linked to its
glassworks, a traditional art that was
imported to Venice from the East
around the year 1000. In 1295, the
Serenissima Republic decreed that
for health and safety reasons the glass
factories would have to leave the city
and Murano, where glassworkers had
already settled, benefitted from the
move. Still today the internationally famous glassworks constitute the
main industry in Murano and are vis-
ited by thousands of tourists, as is the
Museo di Vetro or Glass Museum.
Worth a visit is the church of **Santi
Maria e Donato** (7th-12th century) and that of **San Pietro Martire**
(15th-16th century).

*The church of Santi Maria e
Donato on Murano, built in the
Veneto-Byzantine style, is one of
the oldest churches on the lagoon.*

❶ *View of Murano.*
❷ *Fondamenta dei Vetrai.*
❸ *A glassworker.*
❹ *View of Murano with the clocktower.*
❺ *A kiln for glassworking.*
❻ *Canale Ponte Longo.*
❼ *View of the Canale degli Angeli.*

BURANO

The name of this island also comes from the city of Altinum and specifically the Borean gate. The fame of Burano is linked to its traditional lacemaking and to its small, brightly-painted houses that once marked the "borders" of the property. Not to be missed is a visit to the **Museo del Merletto** or Lace Museum and a stroll past the houses on the island to discover the famous **Casa del Bepi,** a summation of all the colours of the homes in Burano. But don't leave the Island without visiting the church of **San Martino Vesco-vo** with its leaning belltower and without having tasted a *bussolà*, a particular ring-shaped cake.

❶ ❷ ❺ *Fondamenta Pescheria.*
❸ *The typical coloured houses of Burano.*
❹ *Fondamenta Cavanella.*

TORCELLO

It seems that, even before the Altinum refugees arrived, the Romans used to holiday on the island. Torcello however had a different fate than the other islands; after centuries of importance it was gradually abandoned, stripped of all its assets and is now largely uninhabited. Don't miss a visit to the 12th century church of **Santa Fosca**, with its central plan, recognizable from the external portico with elegant white raised columns. Also worth seeing is the recently restored **Ponte del Diavolo** or Devil's Bridge, without a parapet like the oldest Venetian bridges.

LIDO

Up to the second half of the 19th century the only buildings on the Lido were a Benedictine abbey and a Jewish cemetery. But in the late 19th century the beneficial properties of seawater were discovered and "bathing" invented. This fashion was immediately taken up in this long and narrow sandbar marking the boundary between the Venice lagoon and the sea. The first bathing establishment was opened in 1857 and from that time on the Lido beaches became a great attraction and not only for Venetians. Art Nouveau buildings appeared and the Lido became a fashionable beach resort where the European élite spent their summer months. A very particular atmosphere which can be relived with the annual **Venice Film Festival** when international stars flock to the Lido. There are also public beaches such as **San Nicolò**, **Alberoni** (a WWF protected oasis) and **Murazzi**. But the private bathing establishments are also worth a visit, with their gaily coloured huts and wide verandas.

Previous page:
Above: the church of Santa Fosca di Torcello has a central plan defined by an
orthogonal porch
Below: The Devil's Bridge on Torcello, a typical Venetian structure dating back to
the 15th century
On this page: Aerial view of the Venice Lido

32R 31R

LEFT BANK

1L	PUNTA DELLA DOGANA		
	E DOGANA DA MAR	PAG.	160
2L	CHIESA DELLA SALUTE	"	160
3L	PALAZZO GENOVESE	"	160
4L	PALAZZO BARBARO	"	162
5L	CA' DARIO	"	162
6L	PALAZZO VENIER DEI LEONI	"	162
7L	PALAZZO BARBARIGO	"	164
8L	PALAZZO LOREDAN CINI	"	164
9L	SCUOLA GRANDE		
	DI S. MARIA DELLA CARITÀ	"	164
9L	GALLERIE DELL'ACCADEMIA	"	164
10L	PALAZZO CONTARINI		
	DEGLI SCRIGNI	"	166
11L	PALAZZO LOREDAN		
	DELL'AMBASCIATORE	"	166
12L	PALAZZO BON REZZONICO	"	166
13L	PALAZZI GIUSTINIAN	"	166
14L	PALAZZO FOSCARI	"	168
15L	PALAZZO BALBI	"	168
16L	PALAZZO PISANI MORETTA	"	170
17L	CA' BARBARIGO		
	DELLA TERRAZZA	"	170
18L	PALAZZO GRIMANI MARCELLO	"	170
19L	PALAZZO BERNARDO	"	170
20L	PALAZZO COCCINA		
	TIEPOLO PAPADOPOLI	"	172
21L	PALAZZO CAMERLENGHI	"	174
22L	FABBRICHE VECCHIE DI RIALTO	"	174
23L	FABBRICHE NUOVE DI RIALTO	"	174
24L	LOGGIA DELLA PESCARIA	"	176
25L	PALAZZO CORNER		
	DELLA REGINA	"	176
26L	CA' PESARO	"	176
27L	SAN STAE	"	176
28L	PALAZZO BELLONI BATTAGIA	"	178
29L	FONDACO DEI TURCHI	"	178

15L 14R
14L 13R
12R
13L
11R
12L
11R 10R
9R
11L
10L

SAILING ALONG **THE GRAND CANAL**

RIGHT BANK

1R	PALAZZO GIUSTINIAN	PAG. 161
2R	PALAZZO BADOER TIEPOLO	" 161
3R	PALAZZO CONTARINI FASAN	" 161
4R	PALAZZO PISANI GRITTI	" 161
5R	PALAZZO BARBARIGO MINOTTO	" 163
6R	PALAZZO CORNER DELLA CA' GRANDA	" 163
7R	PALAZZO PISANI	" 165
8R	PALAZZO BARBARO A SAN VIDAL	" 165
9R	PALAZZO FALIER CANOSSA	" 167
10R	CA' DEL DUCA	" 167
11R	PALAZZO GRASSI	" 167
12R	PALAZZO MORO LIN	" 167
13R	PALAZZO ERIZZO NANI MOCENIGO	" 169
14R	PALAZZO CONTARINI DALLE FIGURE	" 169
15R	PALAZZO MOCENIGO CASA VECCHIA	" 169
16R	PALAZZO MOCENIGO CASA NUOVA	" 169
17R	PALAZZO CORNER SPINELLI	" 171
18R	PALAZZO GRIMANI	" 173
19R	PALAZZO DANDOLO FARSETTI	" 173
20R	PALAZZO CORNER LOREDAN	" 173
21R	PALAZZO BEMBO	" 173
22R	PALAZZO DOLFIN MANIN	" 173
23R	FONDACO DEI TEDESCHI	" 175
24R	PALAZZO DA MOSTO	" 175
25R	PALAZZO MICHIEL DAL BRUSÀ	" 175
26R	PALAZZO MICHIEL DALLE COLONNE	" 175
27R	PALAZZO SAGREDO	" 177
28R	CA' D'ORO	" 177
29R	PALAZZO LOREDAN GRIMANI VENDRAMIN CALERGI	" 179
30R	SANTA MARCUOLA	" 179
31R	CHIESA DI SAN GEREMIA	" 179
32R	PALAZZO FLANGINI	" 179

3 L - PALAZZO GENOVESE

Built in 1892 by the architect *Tricomi Mattei* in the Venetian neo-Gothic style is the residence of the Genovese family. It was transformed into a luxury hotel in 2009.

1 L - PUNTA DELLA DOGANA AND DOGANA DA MAR

The Punta della Dogana stands between the Grand Canal and the Giudecca Canal. The Dogana da Mar was built around 1677 by the architect *Giuseppe Benoni*. Goods entering Venice by sea were unloaded and cleared through customs here.

2 L - CHIESA DELLA SALUTE

Built following a solemn vow by Doge *Nicolò Contarini* after the terrible plague of 1630, the building was designed by *Baldassarre Longhena*. It has a central octagonal plan and is covered by a large dome. The exterior has imposing vaulted buttresses.

4 R - PALAZZO PISANI GRITTI

Built in the early 15th century, the palace has four stories with a very low ground floor and three upper floors all in the Gothic style with lancet windows. The building is now a hotel.

3 R - PALAZZO CONTARINI FASAN

This small palace dates back to the 15th century. It has a facade divided into three sections. Legend has it that it was the home of *Desdemona*, Othello's tragic wife of Shakespearian fame.

2 R - PALAZZO BADOER TIEPOLO

It was built on the alleged site of a Byzantine structure. The double water entrance (access from the water to the building for people and goods in boats) reveals that it was a two-family residence.

1 R - PALAZZO GIUSTINIAN

The palace was built in the second half of the 15th century. In 1820 it was transformed into a hotel where famous personalities such as *Théophile Gautier*, *Marcel Proust* and *Giuseppe Verdi* stayed. After the Municipality acquired it, the palace was extensively renovated and now houses the **Venice Biennale** offices.

6 L - PALAZZO VENIER DEI LEONI

Commissioned by the Venier family in 1749, *Lorenzo Boschetti* created an imposing and monumental palace although work stopped after the first story was built and it was never finished. It has a broad landing stage leading to the central loggia with its three great arches. The palace once belonged to *Peggy Guggenheim* and now houses her personal art collection.

4 L - PALAZZO BARBARO

The six-light mullioned window on the first floor dating back to the mid 15th century stands out for its originality and linearity. In 1894 *Eleonora Duse* lived in the upper floor of the palace.

5 L - CA' DARIO

In this palace of Gothic origin, the Renaissance facade of 1487 is of particular interest, with its precious coloured marble roundels of set in Istrian stone.

6 R - PALAZZO CORNER DELLA CA' GRANDA

Designed by *Jacopo Sansovino* in 1533, it has a facade divided into two horizontal bands: the lower is decorated with rustication and the upper with a series of arches with wide balcony windows. Sold to the State in 1812 it now houses the Prefecture.

5 R - PALAZZO BARBARIGO MINOTTO

Built in the 15th century in the Venetian Gothic style, during the first half of the 18th century it was embellished by the work of numerous artists, including Tiepolo, Fontebasso and Mingozzi. It now hosts the prestigious **Musica a Palazzo concerts.**

9 L - SCUOLA GRANDE DI S. MARIA DELLA CARITÀ
GALLERIE DELL'ACCADEMIA

In front of the Accademia Bridge is the S. Maria della Carità complex, made up of a church, monastery and school. The Accademia Art Gallery was set up in this latter building at the end of the 18th century. The gallery now takes up the entire complex and houses the most complete collection of Venetian painting ranging from the 14th to the 19th centuries.

8 L - PALAZZO LOREDAN CINI

The building is a typical example of the mid 16th-century classical style.

7 L - PALAZZO BARBARIGO

Erected in the 16th century, the palace is distinguished by its 19th century mosaics of Murano glass after cartoons by *G. Carlini*. In the late 19th century it housed the **Compagnia di Venezia e Murano**, consisting of glass and mosaic factory proprietors who decided to redesign the Grand Canal facade.

8 R - PALAZZO BARBARO A SAN VIDAL

It consists of two buildings. The older one, Palazzo Barbaro Curtis, dates back to the first half of the 15th century. The second was a late 17th-century extension and used to boast decorations by *Tiepolo*, now unhappily lost. The palaces have been owned by the Curtis family since the mid 19th century which, besides restoring them, also gave hospitality to the famous writer *Henry James*.

7 R - PALAZZO PISANI

This small palace was purchased by the wealthy Pisani family in 1751. The marble coat-of-arms of the family, with a lion rampant, is visible between the two double lancet windows on the *piano nobile*.

During the last war, the building was the residence of the Duca di Genova and was then occupied by the allied command. Today it once again belongs to the Pisani family.

13 L - PALAZZO GIUSTINIAN

Although it seems a single edifice from the outside, this elegant Gothic palace is really two separate residences dating back to 1452. *Richard Wagner* lived here in 1858 where he composed a part of **Tristan und Isolde**.

12 L - CA' REZZONICO

The imposing and spectacular palace built for the noble Bon family in 1649 by *B. Longhena* was only completed in the mid 18th century by *G. Massari*, when it was acquired by the Rezzonico family. It now houses the **Venetian Musum of 18th Century Art.**

11 L - PALAZZO LOREDAN DELL'AMBASCIATORE

A late 15th-century Gothic palace with typical Venetian elements, such as the loggia on the *piano nobile* very similar to that of the Doges' Palace and Ca' d'Oro. In the 18th century it was the residence of the Austrian empire's ambassadors, hence its name.

10 L - PALAZZO CONTARINI DEGLI SCRIGNI

This is a pair of adjoining palaces. The first (on the left) in the late Gothic style and the second (on the right) was built by *Vincenzo Scamozzi* in 1609. One of its owners, *Girolamo Contarini*, left his valuable paintings to the Gallerie dell'Accademia.

12 R - PALAZZO MORO LIN

The palace was built around 1670 and has a symmetrical facade with four orders. It is also called "house of the thirteen windows".

11 R - PALAZZO GRASSI

This is one of the finest examples of 18th.century buildings designed by *G. Massari* in 1749 for the Grassi family. Since 1984 it has belonged to the FIAT group (who had it restored by *Gae Aulenti* and *Antonio Foscari*). It was sold in 2005 to *François Pinault*, who exhibits his personal art collection here.

10 R - CA' DEL DUCA

The construction of this palace was begun by *Francesco Sforza* Duke of Milan in 1461 but the Republic sequestrated the property when the work stopped. *Titian* had his studio here in 1514.

9 R - PALAZZO FALIER CANOSSA

This 15th-century palace stands out for its two projecting wings with their enclosed balconies (*liagò*). The *piano nobile* has a loggia consisting of a row of arches in the Venetian-Gothic style on Corinthian columns. The palace is still a private residence.

15 L - PALAZZO BALBI

The palace dates back to 1582 and was designed by the architect *Alessandro Vittoria*. The owner Nicolò Balbi, who during the works resided on a boat, never lived here since he died before it was completed. It is currently the seat of the **Veneto Region.**

14 L - CA' FOSCARI

One of the finest palaces of the city, it constitutes a notable example of the Venetian Gothic style. Originally belonging to the Giustinian family, it passed through various hands up to 1452, when Doge Foscari bought it at auction. Today it is the seat of the University of Venice.

16 R - PALAZZO MOCENIGO CASA NUOVA

The building, dating back to the second half of the 15th century, was completed at the beginning of the 17th century. *Byron* lived here in 1818 and wrote the first part of **Don Juan;** his lover threw herself from its terrace.

15 R - PALAZZO MOCENIGO CASA VECCHIA

Giordano Bruno lived in the palace, rebuilt in the first half of the 17th century to a design by *Francesco Contin*, until his host Giovanni Mocenigo reported him to the Santo Uffizio.

14 R - PALAZZO CONTARINI DALLE FIGURE

Built in the first half of the 16th century, its name comes from the two figures (caryatids) above the entrance. *Andrea Palladio* lived here.

13 R - PALAZZO ERIZZO NANI MOCENIGO

Built for the Erizzo family in 1480, this elegant palace has many typical Venetian Gothic elements. It was later acquired by the Passò Nani Mocenigo family.

19 L - PALAZZO BERNARDO

Begun in the early 15th century, it has two doorways opening on to the canal (see Palazzo Badoer Tiepolo, p. 161) testifying to the fact that two families probably lived here. The first two floors are completely asymmetrical.

18 L - PALAZZO GRIMANI MARCELLO

One of the first palaces of the Venetian Renaissance, built to a design by *Giovanni Buora.*

16 L - PALAZZO PISANI MORETTA

The mid 15th-century facade of this palace has two floors of six-light mullioned windows and two central doorways opening on to the canal on the ground floor.

17 L - CA' BARBARIGO DELLA TERRAZZA

Initiated around 1568, the works were interrupted and the structure was finished with a vast terrace that gives the palace its name.

17 R - PALAZZO CORNER SPINELLI

Built around 1490 by *Mauro Codussi*, the interior of the 16th-century building was modernised by *Michele Sanmicheli* who made it a clear example of the passage from the Gothic style to the new Renaissance lines.

Below: Mars and Venus by Giambattista Tiepolo in the Palazzo Pisani Moretta

20 L - PALAZZO COCCINA TIEPOLO PAPADOPOLI

Built around the mid 16th century in a traditional Venetian style, it has a finely proportioned facade with large windows. The garden was created in the 19th century.

Below: interior of Palazzo Grimani.

22 R - PALAZZO DOLFIN MANIN

Dating back to the 16th century, it was the residence of the last Doge *Ludovico Manin*. The facade is by *Jacopo Sansovino*. It is currently the seat of the **Bank of Italy**.

21 R - PALAZZO BEMBO

Built by the patrician Bembo family in the 15th century, it was frequently altered over the centuries, especially inside. Pietro Bembo, Venetian writer, grammarian and humanist was born here in 1470.

20 R - PALAZZO CORNER LOREDAN

Constructed in the 13th century as a *casa-fondaco* it was later extended and altered. In 1362 the king of Cyprus lived there and 1868 the Municipality of Venice acquired it. It still houses the municipal offices.

19 R - PALAZZO DANDOLO FARSETTI

Erected in the 13th century by the heirs of Doge Enrico Dandolo, it then passed to the Farsetti family and later still became a hotel for a brief period. Since 1826 it has been owned by the Municipality of Venice which has its seat here.

18 R - PALAZZO GRIMANI

It was the home of a branch of the Grimani family up to 1806. It later became the property of the State and seat of the Main Post Office. It now houses the Venice Appeal Court.

23 L - FABBRICHE NUOVE DI RIALTO

The Fabbriche Nuove were built in the 16th century and designed by *Jacopo Sansovino* for the mercantile magistrates. The long building on the Grand Canal has a rusticated portico on its front; the first and second floors are divided by pilasters with windows between them.

21 L - PALAZZO CAMERLENGHI

The building is distinguished by the inclination of the two consecutive facades that follow the shore of the canal. The main facade is that facing the Rialto Bridge. In the 16th century the lower floor was used as a jail for tax evaders and the upper floors housed the State Treasury.

22 L - FABBRICHE VECCHIE DI RIALTO

In 1513 a fire destroyed most of the Rialto markets. The architect Scarpagnino drew up a new town plan that included long, two-story buildings with arcades like the Fabbriche Vecchie. The ground floor houses shops and warehouses, the upper floor the magistrates' offices and activities linked to the market and commerce.

THE GRAND CANAL

26 R - PALAZZO MICHIEL DALLE COLONNE

The 18th-century interventions gave this Gothic-Byzantine palace its current aspect. Its name comes from the Byzantine columns on its facade.

25 R - PALAZZO MICHIEL DAL BRUSÀ

Palazzo Bianchi Michiel or Palazzo Michiel dal Brusà was built on the site of a Gothic palace destroyed by a fire (hence its name *brusà* - burnt) in 1774.

24 R - CA' DA MOSTO

Despite its frequent alterations, this building still preserves the aspect of the 13th-century *casa-fondaco*. It is the birthplace of *Alvise Cadamosto*, Venetian explorer employed by Portugal from 1454 to 1462. From the 16th to 18th centuries the palace was transformed into a hotel, the **Leone Bianco**, one of the most famous in the city.

23 R - FONDACO DEI TEDESCHI

The original 13th-century building was designed as a warehouse for the goods brought here by German merchants. It was destroyed by a fire in 1505 and immediately rebuilt to designs by *Girolamo Tedesco*. The spaces between the windows boasted frescoes by *Giorgione and Titian*, now unfortunately lost.

27 L - CHIESA DI SAN STAE

The church, whose name is a dialect abbreviation of *St. Eustachius*, dates back to the 10th century. The building, initially a Veneto-Byzantine structure, was rebuilt in the 18th century so that the new church would face the canal. It has an impressive entrance.

26 L - CA' PESARO

This is a magnificent example of Venetian baroque, begun by *Longhena* in 1628. The Grand Canal facade is spectacular and the ground floor has a bold diamond rustication. The building now houses the **Museo d'Arte Moderna e di Arte Orientale**.

25 L - PALAZZO CORNER DELLA REGINA

The facade has rustication on the ground floor and mezzanine, with the water door in the centre, flanked by windows and another two low entrances. Both the upper floors are characterized by columns in high relief.

24 L - LOGGIA DELLA PESCARIA

This neo-Gothic building with its arcades dates back to 1907. The ground floor housed the fish market, with offices on the first floor. The fish stalls were then moved to the ground floor of the building at the back, overlooking the campo delle Beccarie.

28 R - CA' D'ORO

The name of this palace comes from the gilt decorations which once adorned its walls. It is undoubtedly one of the most representative examples of Gothic Venetian architecture. The palace was completed in 1440.

27 R - PALAZZO SAGREDO

Built in the late 15th-ventury Gothic-Venetian style, the facade has a particular architectural composition that creates enchanting light effects inside. Today it is a luxury hotel.

29 L - FONDACO DEI TURCHI

The original building dates back to the 13th century. It had a ground floor with ten arches between two angle towers and continuous windows on the first floor. Brick crenulations crowned the central part of the facade. After various vicissitudes, including its use by the Turks, in 1869 it underwent a restoration that radically altered the character of one of the most interesting Byzantine *fondaco* buildings. Today it houses the **Museo di Storia Naturale**.

28 L - PALAZZO BELLONI BATTAGIA

In the mid 17th century *Girolamo Belloni* entrusted the design of this palace to *Baldassare Longhena*. Unfortunately, when the work was finished Belloni ran out of money and he was forced to rent the house to *Conte Czernin*. The palace has a typically baroque facade with two symmetrical, obelisk-shaped pinnacles on the roof.

32 R - PALAZZO FLANGINI

The ancient Gothic building was acquired in 1638 by the wealthy lawyer *Tommaso Flangini*, who completely renovated it. *G. Sardi* is responsible for its Renaissance character with the fine doorway and two great balconies.

31 R - CHIESA DI SAN GEREMIA

The initial church, later rebuilt, dates back to the 11th century. The current building was designed by Carlo Corbellini in 1753. The brick belltower is one of the oldest in Venice. The body of St. Lucy, one of the most venerated Christian saints, is enshrined inside.

30 R - CHIESA DI SAN MARCUOLA

Erected in the 12th century, the first church was set lengthwise to the Grand Canal and had a *campo* in front. The structure was in the Romanesque style with its nave and two aisles and trussed roof. After its restoration In the 18th century by *Giorgio Massari* it had a single nave with a square plan covered by a barrel vault. Worth viewing inside is Tintoretto's **Last Supper**.

29 R - PALAZZO LOREDAN GRIMANI VENDRAMIN CALERGI

A Renaissance building by *Mauro Codussi* it passed to the Calergi family, who had the right wing of the palace enlarged, and then to the Vendramins. In 1658 a nobleman was assassinated in the right wing, called Ala Grimani, after which this part of the building was razed to the ground. It was rebuilt in 1883 and *Richard Wagner* lived here for a year until his death.

The mask of the Venice Carnival

The symbol of the Venetian carnival is the mask that serves to hide any difference between social classes and gives a sense of freedom from the pressures of daily life.

The Venetian costume *par excellence* is the *bauta* and dates back to the 18th century. Worn by men and women it consists of a white mask (the *larva*), a three-cornered hat and a dark cloak. This outfit was also used in romantic meetings and at parties, since the shape of the mask enabled the wearer to eat and drink without removing it. Another typical Venetian costume was the *gnaga*, where men dressed as women wore a mask with feline features and carried a basket with a kitten inside it. For their part the women often dressed in the *moretta* costume, that is a small, black velvet mask with a hat and elegant clothes.

A particularity of the mask was that of making people "dumb", because it was kept in place by biting on a small support attached to the mask.

Another traditional mask was the **mattaccino**, a clown wearing a short white or multi-coloured dress and a feathered hat, who throws perfumed eggs at friends and young girls in love. Alongside these traditional masks are the typical ones of the **Commedia dell'Arte,** made famous in Italy and the world by the comedies of Carlo Goldoni. In recent years the Carnival of Venice has returned to its ancient splendour.

Once a year, a lively and brightly coloured crowd of people in costume pours into the *calli* and *campi* for the excitement of children and adults, of tourists and of Venetians.

Carnival Masks

Mattacino   Moretta   Bauta

Fisherman of Chioggia   Domino costume   Larva or Volto

Gnaga

Plague doctor

The Doctor

Brighella

Pantaloon

Harlequin

183

①

②

Venetian Cuisine

Fish plays a fundamental role in Venetian cuisine, and especially the risottos with *peoci* (mussels), *cape* (seafood), scampi, *bisato* (eel) or cuttlefish. Fish is also roasted on the *grea* (griglia) or, even better, fried, such as the typical *moeca*, small crabs caught and eaten during the phase changes when they are soft. Not to be forgotten are the *sarde in saor*, sardines marinated in onion and vinegar and then fried or *bacalà* (dried salt cod) Venetian style: soaked for hours in milk and flour. But if we're speaking about Venice and its cuisine we have to mention the market gardens of Murano and the larger islands, from where come the *bisi* (peas) cooked with rice (*risi e* bisi) or the beans for the equally famous *pasta e fasioi*.

1. **Sopa de Pesse** *(fish soup). Prepared with the day's catch; sometimes served with toast.*
2. **Gnochi de patate** *(potato dumplings). It is traditional to eat them on the last Friday of Carnival.*

3. **Gransipori a'la venessiana** *(Venetian crabs). They have a delicate taste and are served boiled or with sauces.*
4. **Sardele in saòr** *(marinated sardines). The saòr is an onion-based marinade served with the sardines.*

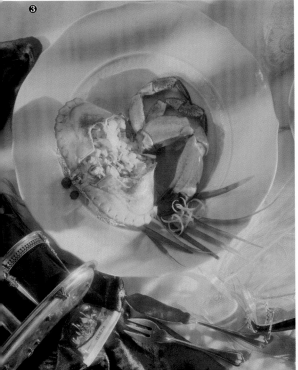

❸

❹

Not to mention the artichokes (*articiochi*), radishes and Trevignano radicchio. Other traditional dishes are *risoto in cavroman,* based on lamb and tomatoes, *risoto a la sbiraglia* with boiled chicken and cheese and *fongadina*, stewed lungs with polenta. Just as traditional are the *castradina* (smoked mutton) and *pinocada* (a cake made with corn flour, pine nuts and currants). Desserts include *frìtole*, fritters with raisins, *galani,* fried pastry ribbons, and *bubana*, a pudding made of pastry leftovers. Not to mention the *storti of* Dolo, small cones of puff pastry, and *baìcoli*, thin biscuits much loved by Giuseppe Verdi and still sold as a Venetian specialty.

5. **Risi e bisi** *(rice and peas). A traditional dish of the Serenissima Republic of Venice, it was offered to the doge on 25 April, St Mark's feastday*
6. **Risoto Nero** *(black risotto). The intense flavour of rice cooked with fish and cuttlefish is inimitable*
7. **Baca'la mantecato** *(dried salt cod). A simple dish which Venetian experience has transformed into a delicacy.*

8. **Figà a'la venessiana** *(liver Venetian style). The Venetians have lightened the strong taste of liver with onions, creating a famous dish*
9. **Carpaccio.** *This is based on finely sliced raw beef fillet dressed with a delicate sauce*
10. **Zabajòn** *(Zabaione). Because of its invigorating properties, it used to be offered to the bridegroom at the end of the wedding feast.*

INDEX

Arsenal 144
Bell tower 71
St Mark's Basilica.....................51
Bridges:
Accademia Bridge.................39
Bridge of Sighs 74
Costituzione Bridge..............43
Rialto Bridge........................41
Scalzi Bridge........................42
Burano 153
Campo San Boldo 95
Campo San Polo......................93
Canal Grande 14
Churches:
Gesuiti 116
Pietà 142
San Geremia 179
San Giacometto 98
San Giacomo dell'Orio 109
San Marcuola.......................179
San Moisè.............................79
San Nicolò dei Mendicoli 133
San Simeone Piccolo.............36
San Stae 30-176
San Zaccaria 142
San Zan Degolà 109
Santa Maria dei Miracoli......115
Santa Maria del Giglio..........80
Santa Maria della Salute . 122-160
Santa Maria di Nazareth
called of the Scalzi...............112
Santa Maria Gloriosa
dei Frari 88
San Rocco.............................86
Tolentini 106
Clocktower...............................61
Coffee House 74
Columns 73
Fabbriche Nuove di Rialto.......174
Fabbriche Vecchie di Rialto 174
La Fenice Theatre 82

Fondaco dei Tedeschi 175
Fondaco dei Turchi............ 34-178
Gallerie dell'Accademia ... 128-164
Ghetto....................................118
Gondolas...................................21
Guggenheim Museum.............126
Historical Regatta....................19
Island of San Giorgio................76
Lido 157
Loggia della Pescaria..............176
Marciana Library......................72
Murano 148
Palaces:
Badoer Tiepolo 161
Balbi 168
Barbarigo 164
Barbarigo Minotto...............163
Barbaro 162
Barbaro a San Vidal 165
Belloni Battagia.............. 35-178
Bembo 173
Bernardo.............................170
Ca' Barbarigo della Terrazza..170
Ca' da Mosto 175
Ca' del Duca 167
Ca' d'Oro...................... 32-177
Ca' Dario 24-162
Ca' Foscari 168
Ca' Pesaro 31-176
Ca' Rezzonico 27-166
Camerlenghi 174
Coccina Tiepolo Papadopoli ..172
Contarini dal Bovolo 80
Contarini dalle Figure..........169
Contarini degli Scrigni.........166
Contarini Fasan 161
Corner della Ca' Granda 163
Corner della Regina 29-176
Corner Loredan 173
Corner Spinelli 171
Dandolo Farsetti 173

Dolfin Manin 173
Ducale 66
Erizzo Nani Mocenigo 169
Falier Canossa 25-167
Flangini 179
Genovese 160
Giustinian............................161
Giustinian............................166
Grassi........................... 26-167
Grimani................................173
Grimani Marcello 170
Loredan Cini 164
Loredan dell'Ambasciatore ...166
Loredan Grimani
Vendramin Calergi........ 37-179
Michiel dal Brusà................175
Michiel dalle Colonne.........175
Mocenigo Casa Nuova.........169
Mocenigo Casa Vecchia 169
Moro Lin 167
Morosini Sagredo.......... 28-177
Pisani...................................165
Pisani Gritti 161
Pisani Moretta 170
Querini Stampalia...............141
Venier dei Leoni.......... 126-162
Procuratie...............................62
Punta della Dogana 160
Rialto and Surroundings.........102
Rialto Markets.........................96
Scuola di San Marco e Santissimi
Giovanni e Paolo 136
Scuola di San Rocco 87
Scuola Grande
di Santa Maria della Carità......164
Scuola Grande di San Giovanni.90
St Mark's Basilica.....................51
St Mark's Square.......................46
Torcello 156